CHANGE AND THE PERSISTENCE OF TRADITION IN INDIA

– FIVE LECTURES –

Edited by

Richard L. Park

Michigan Papers on South and Southeast Asia

Number 2

1971

THE UNIVERSITY OF MICHIGAN
CENTER FOR SOUTH AND SOUTHEAST ASIAN STUDIES

MICHIGAN PAPERS ON SOUTH AND SOUTHEAST ASIA

Editorial Board

John K. Musgrave
George B. Simmons
Thomas R. Trautmann, chm.

Ann Arbor, Michigan

Open access edition funded by the National Endowment for the Humanities/ Andrew W. Mellon Foundation Humanities Open Book Program.

Library of Congress Catalog Card Number 76-635331

Copyright 1971

by

Center for South and Southeast Asian Studies
The University of Michigan
Ann Arbor, Michigan 48104

Printed and bound by CPI Group (UK) Ltd, Croydon, CR0 4YY

ISBN 978-0-472-03843-5 (paper)
ISBN 978-0-472-12826-6 (ebook)
ISBN 978-0-472-90226-2 (open access)

PREFACE

The lectures presented in this volume were given during the summer of 1970 under the sponsorship of the CIC Summer Program on South Asia and the Center for South and Southeast Asian Studies of The University of Michigan. The lecture by A. K. Ramanujan, Professor of Dravidian Studies and Linguistics at The University of Chicago ("The Interior Landscape: The Poetic Tradition in Classical Tamil"), and that by Padmanabha S. Jaini, Professor of Indic Languages and Literatures at The University of Michigan ("Śramaṇas and their Conflict with Brahmanical Society"), cannot be included because of commitments to publication elsewhere.

It should be recognized that these essays appear in revised lecture form, and not as fully polished scholarly papers. They carry nevertheless the authority--and no little verve--of experienced scholars concerned both with the traditions and the changes so characteristic of modern India.

We are grateful to the lecturers for their contributions and for the efforts they expended in preparing their notes for publication.

Richard L. Park

Ann Arbor
1971

CONTENTS

Preface

CONTENTS

The Green Revolution in South Asia

by

Kusum Nair

"A man who is born into a world already possessed,
if he cannot get subsistence from his parents on
whom he has a just demand, and if the society do
not want his labour, has no claim of <u>*right*</u> *to the*
smallest portion of food, and, in fact, has no
business to be where he is. At nature's mighty
feast there is no vacant cover for him."

Robert Malthus

On December 5, 1969, the House Foreign Affairs Sub-committee on National Security Policy and Scientific Developments held a one-day symposium in Washington D. C. devoted to the Green Revolution.

In his opening remarks, the chairman of the Subcommittee, Clement J. Zablocki, described it as a "shorthand phrase," a "slogan," that while "perhaps unscientific in tone . . . expresses graphically the dramatic changes which are taking place in the less developed countries because of the introduction of the high-yield cereal varieties--the so-called miracle grains."[1]

The less developed countries referred to stretch across the three continents of Africa, Asia and Latin America. The so-called "miracle" grains are new varieties of wheat and rice mainly, though improved strains of corn, millets and sorghums also have been developed in recent years. These were introduced into South Asia in the mid-sixties.

The phrase "green revolution" was first used in March 1968, by the then Administrator of U. S. AID, William S. Gaud. It gained instantaneous worldwide currency. According to Mr. Gaud's testimony at this same hearing before the House

Subcommittee: "...by the grace of God and a stroke of tremendous good fortune," --as an aside, it is an unbeatable combination-- "only a few years ago the research activities of the Rockefeller Foundation, the Ford Foundation, and others culminated in the production of the new varieties which produce so much more food than the old."

As to their impact, Mr. Gaud continued:

> Intrinsically, this was a tremendous development. But from the standpoint of someone in the aid business, as I was, it was also important because it added an element of drama, an element of excitement--some sex appeal, if you will--to agricultural production.

> Any man who saw his neighbor using the new seeds could see for himself what they could do. Their use spread rapidly in countries like Turkey, India, Pakistan, and the Philippines because individual farmers could see for themselves what a difference they made.

> The normally complicated business of the development process--how to get a country to develop, how to get people to change their attitudes--suddenly came down to a very simple proposition: one man seeing his neighbor doing better than he was doing. So these seeds had a tremendous effect, and they made the job of increasing food production much easier than it had ever been before.

Mr. Gaud further informed the Subcommittee that "In terms of policy guidance, we tried to persuade the developing countries to adopt and follow policies which would furnish incentives to farmers to grow more food."[2]

In practice, these incentives generally took the form of highly profitable support price guarantees; subsidies on imports like fertilizers, other chemicals, and farm machinery; and no tax on agricultural income!

So much for the background. How does the Green Revolution look on the ground, however? There will not be sufficient time to present the total picture, to state all the facts and problems, or to discuss aspects like the "sex appeal" of the new technology.

In geographic terms, the Green Revolution has made little progress in Africa or Latin America. So far, it has been limited to a few countries, almost all of them in Asia. From less than 5,000 acres in 1966/67, approximately 30 million acres were reportedly planted in Asia to the improved varieties of wheat and rice in 1968/69. Even allowing for gross inaccuracies in estimates, the initial spread was rapid, but not uniformly so--among countries, among regions within a country, and among farms within a region. Moreover, it still represented less than 7 percent of the rice acreage in South and Southeast Asia, and around 20 percent of the wheat lands.[3]

Additional acres are likely to be slower in coming, because aside from a range of other factors, the miracle grains must have adequate and controlled irrigation. A critical variable, it is in acute short supply. Only 20 percent of the rice in the tropical belt is irrigated; and most of it by gravity flow. Storage facilities are usually lacking and the water supply fluctuates with the rainfall. Furthermore, as against the tall native varieties, the new plant types have been bred to be short-stemmed, so they can absorb large inputs of fertilizers without lodging before harvest. The deep water conditions in most parts of India, the flood plains of South Vietnam, central Thailand, and East Pakistan, however, are not suited for dwarfs. They drown. Also, they are much too susceptible to too many diseases.

In the major rice growing countries of tropical Asia, therefore, the miracle of the new rice has not been nearly as spectacular as was anticipated. Progenies of the new Mexican wheat have been more adaptable to local climes and conditions, and have shown greater yield increases than rice.[4] On the whole, however, it would be fair to say that the revolution has not been of as cosmic a significance as acclaimed. Nor has it, in Mr. Gaud's words, suddenly reduced the "normally complicated business of development process to a very simple proposition". Over the world, men have seen their neighbor do better than they since the dawn of history, and for a variety of reasons, failed to do very much about it.

India has the largest acreage of any country under the high yield varieties. The new rice was expected to yield from 50 to 100 percent more than the old strains at their respective maximum potential levels. In 1968, it was planted on 6.5

million acres, on the best lands, and presumably by the best farmers. Yet, the total output of rice in that year was 37.9 million metric tons as against 39.03 million tons in 1965, when no land had been sown to the miracle rice. It increased to 39.76 million tons in the following year, but so did the acreage, by 1.5 million acres above that of 1965. Increase in wheat production was sizeable over the same period--six million tons more in 1969 than four years earlier. But the acreage also had increased by six million acres.

Moreover, as against 91.3 million acres under rice in India, the total acreage in wheat is only 39.4 million (1968-69). As in the rest of Asia, rice is the most important food crop. A significant breakthrough in its production, however, has yet to be made. Despite the impressive spread of the new seeds since 1966, in fact, instead of an anticipated dramatic increase in output that was to have made the country self-sufficient by 1971, food grain production has been below the corresponding estimates (by 6.5 million tons for 1968-69) based on past trends computed for the pre-Green Revolution era of 1951-65. Consequently, the national goal of eliminating all imports of cereals has been postponed to 1974. By then, the area under the new varieties is expected to triple over that in 1969, and yield two-thirds of the additional output.

2

Whereas the promise of abundance is yet to be realized, and it will bring with it its own severe problems, like marketing, the Green Revolution is creating other grave distortions in countries of South Asia. In India, for instance, approximately three-fourths of the cultivated land is precluded from adopting the new varieties because it is not irrigated. More serious perhaps, a new structure of agricultural organization and techniques is being introduced. Its impact in the rural and urban areas on distribution of production assets, incomes and employment, and on economic and social relationships, will have considerable political ramifications.

It is well established by now, that the benefits flowing from the cultivation of new varieties have been limited to a very narrow strata of large farmers with substantial holdings of land,

resources, and easy access to credit. The benefits are pre-
dominantly not from higher yields alone, but from the inordi-
nately high prices that governments have been persuaded to
guarantee farmers as incentives to cultivate the new seeds. For
wheat, in India and Pakistan, the support price has been roughly
double the world market price and what farmers in the major
exporting countries were receiving.

According to one survey, among wheat farmers in north
India, those with holdings of ten acres or less have experienced
a substantial relative deterioration in their economic condition.
Yet, in the Gangetic wheat belt stretching across the states of
Uttar Pradesh and Bihar, over 80 percent of the farm households operate less than 8 acres. In rice growing areas the
situation is far worse. The overwhelming majority of the
cultivators have infinitely smaller holdings or no land at all.
The over-all estimate is that farmers with 20 acres or more
have made the greatest absolute and relative gains. In India,
however, 95 percent of the farm households own less than 20
acres each, of all types, irrigated and otherwise, though
together it constitutes 64 percent of the cultivated acreage.

Wherever the Green Revolution has made a significant
impact, in fact, it has benefited a very small minority of the
population in a few regions only. It has and continues to widen
income disparities between regions, and between the few large
and wealthy farmers on the one hand, and the great mass of
peasants, tenants, and the landless within the areas using the
new techniques. The small cultivator lacks generally the
motivation and/or the means to invest in irrigation, or to
purchase the manufactured inputs, like fertilizer, pesticides
or equipment, required for the "miracle" seeds. Cultivation
costs of the new varieties are significantly higher than of the
old.

It is not that a vast gap between the rural rich and the poor
did not exist prior to the Green Revolution. But it is becoming
more sharply accentuated since, and is more visible and
disruptive. Hitherto, for instance, the large and upper caste
group of landowners were, as a rule, renting the greater part
of their land to several tenants and share-croppers. If they
retained any portion, it was cultivated by hired wage labor. The
average size of an operational holding for all India in 1961 was

6.5 acres.[5] Although ownership of property was highly skewed, income from the produce of the land was nevertheless shared among several families, in whatever the proportions.

Since the introduction of the new seeds, however, rents have risen sharply. Land values have sky-rocketed--three, four, even five-fold, and more. Landlords are scrambling to resume the leased out land for self-cultivation, both because it is highly profitable now, and to safeguard their title to the property in case the government should decide to enforce more drastic tenancy reforms.

Furthermore, in order to farm more extensively, with less cost perhaps, and with troubles of labor supervision and management, medium and large landowners are mechanizing as rapidly as possible. The taboo that prevented the Brahman or Rajput from plowing with bullocks does not apply to his driving a tractor. On the contrary, it has become a status symbol. Farmers owning ten and fifteen acres are purchasing 35 hp tractors.

And so, in 1969 there were 90,000 tractors in India as against 31,000 in 1961. The current annual demand is estimated at 70,000. It is expected to increase to 90,000 a year over the next couple of years. The bulk of these machines are in the range of 30 to 50 horsepower. Other tillage equipment, including self-propelled combines, are being imported under loan agreements with the World Bank to expedite the process of total mechanization of all operations from sowing to harvest, and not just plowing.

Given the choice and availability, there is every reason to expect that the larger farmers will further intensify and expand their operations by employing labor-saving farm machinery rather than labor. They will do so if the profits remain as attractive as now, and even if they should decline. Yet, for just tractor mechanization to be economic in northern India, for instance, it is computed that a farm should have more than 40 acres. It means that not a single state could mechanize its agriculture economically without considerably enlarging the existing average operational unit. Even in the Punjab, this is only 9.5 acres. And that is precisely what is happening. Whereas tenants are being ejected to join the ranks of the landless, the larger farmers are purchasing more land. Since no arable land remains uncultivated, they can do so only from their smaller and weaker neighbors.

In short, in the medium and long run, farm labor is threatened with massive displacement in the absence of any off-setting non-farm job opportunities. As a very first step in this process, however, if only the less-than-five-acre farms are eliminated, around 250 million people would be on the road in India alone. The question is, where will they go, and what will they do? The city slums will not have the living space, nor will industry or any other sector of the economy have the capacity to absorb such a large addition to its work force. It would be a remarkable achievement, in fact, if the urban sector were able to provide adequate housing and employment opportunities for the natural increase in its own population for the better part of a century.

3

In awarding the Nobel Peace Prize for 1970 to the American agronomist, Norman E. Borlaug, it was stated that "the green revolution has made it possible for the developing countries to break away from hunger and poverty...to abolish hunger...."

If present agricultural policies continue, however, even if India were to quadruple her food production immediately, the majority of her population would still face extremes of abject poverty and starvation. It would not have the means to purchase the food. Neither poverty nor hunger would have been abolished. With surplus in storage, the poor could be placed on dole -- given free food stamps. But can any nation put the majority of its people on a dole and expect to survive economically, socially, or politically?

Moreover, it is not as if the problems of displacement of farm labor and employment will end with just one, the present, generation. Its children, and their children, will not be able to secure jobs either, even if they obtained more education than their parents. At the same time, an increasing concentration of production roles, incomes, and assets will continue relentlessly to push people out of the rural areas.

Leading development theorists nevertheless view these trends and prospects not only as inevitable and inherent in the growth process, but of peripheral relevance and essentially outside the main stream of economic analysis and policy. Imbalances, including a widening of income disparities, are expected to accompany radical innovations and change in production techniques as involved in the cultivation of the new seeds.

And yet, somehow, in a country with over half its population at a per capita level of consumption of less than $32 p.a. (India, 1967-68), a development strategy that must further increase income disparities and unemployment does not appear to make much sense, even if it be good economics. The fact that monstrous inequities in the distribution of wealth and power have been historically an integral characteristic of Indian, as of other South and Southeast Asian societies, and cannot therefore be blamed on the Green Revolution, is no argument for making them worse, in defense precisely of "progress." It would be in conflict not only with the moral and political framework of the Indian Constitution, for instance, with its commitment to democracy, social justice, and egalitarianism, but with the central purpose surely of development itself.

Severe tensions and violence in the countryside are already threatening political stability and orderly economic development and progress nationally. The traditional authority patterns, work obligations, and customary relationships between landlords, tenants, and laborers, also are eroding. When displacement of the farm population reaches a crisis dimension, it will not lend itself to any rational or orderly solution. No government will be able to contain it by belated reform and welfare legislation and a more stringent enforcement of law and order.

The resulting disequilibria could create a revolutionary climate, culminating in a messy, violent, and total reorganization of the agrarian society. Since the crisis can be anticipated, however, would it not be prudent to induce and, if necessary, compel the rural classes in the upper income strata to surrender peacefully most of their landed property, and to control production technology and scale of farming to subserve the demographic and resource endowments of the country before the situation becomes irreversible?

4

The legacy of random fortuitous forces, of history and
birth, a given pattern of private ownership of land is no more
timeless or unalterable than the nature of an economic and
cultural system. Nor can development policy be detached from
the nature and concrete realities of the human society it is
seeking to transform. These are given and dictate the
imperatives of priorities and goals.

In South Asia today, issues of equity and employment in the
rural areas cannot be consigned to the poor house as illegitimate
offsprings of induced technical change; to the realm of social
and political, and not economic, action. It is important to
understand that increase in food production in these countries
is not required merely to eliminate imports to save foreign
exchange. It is required as urgently, or even more so, to
improve the purchasing power and standard of living of the rural
masses within agriculture. In India, they constitute around
80 percent of the population. They are the bulk of the consumers;
the domestic market, not only for food, but for industrial
products as well. And their poverty is as staggering as their
numbers.

On the other hand, the rural élites in South Asia are rel-
atively few in numbers, and have the education, skills, and
resources to invest in other sectors, like trading or manufac-
turing. They could also enter the services. If a small farm
with a pair of bullocks, or a two or five horsepower tiller is
too modest for their aspirations, they could use their talents
elsewhere in a manner that would be gainful to them and to the
economy. They will not have to sleep on the pavements of
Bombay, Calcutta, Dacca, or Karachi, or depend on charity
in order to stay alive.

Agricultural growth and equitable distribution of its fruits
will have to be treated therefore as aspects of one and the same
process. Efforts to deal with one to the exclusion of the other,
sequentially, have never succeeded even in developed countries
like the United States. Furthermore, there is no reason why
small scale farming cannot be made scientific and highly productive in terms of yields per unit of land. Neither the average
density of agricultural working population, nor the net product

per unit of land in South Asia, is nearly as high as in Japan, for instance. [6] "Neither <u>large</u> machines nor <u>large</u> farms are indispensable to 'modernity' or efficiency in agriculture."[7]

Despite much rhetoric to the contrary, current development policies are structured to encourage the upper landed classes to expand production through a virtually unrestricted use of private property and technology and through the mechanism of a market and other auxiliary services stacked heavily in their favor. Under these circumstances, enough commercial farmers will possibly be found in these countries to achieve an adequate increase in aggregate production. The impact of such a situation on the subsequent pattern and spread of production opportunities, income, and employment, however, would be indefensible in densely populated agrarian economies where land is the primary limiting factor. Unless countered by firm government intervention, it will create a greater differential in the economic structure, a narrower base of production, and a social hierarchy and stratification in rural society worse than the prevalent divisions on traditional lines of tribe, caste, and class.

In the long run, the strategy cannot but culminate, as in the West, in the expropriation of the means of livelihood and social status of the peasantry; its total disintegration, death, and destruction. A somewhat similar process in more recent times led to an outmigration of some 25 million farm people in the United States between 1940 and 1965. At that, it has not been sufficient to offset the inflow of new capital and technology that continues to render an increasing number of farmers obsolete and surplus.

If only the cultivators owning less than 20 acres were to be forced similarly to quit agriculture in India, as a consequence of technical changes involving adoption of sophisticated, costly, labor-saving machines, like 50 hp self-propelled combines, they would number, as of now, some 340 million people!

If that be "progress," then with due apologies to Ibsen, it would be like sailing with a cargo of corpses.

TABLE 1

USE OF NEW CEREAL VARIETIES,
SOUTH AND SOUTHEAST ASIA

Rice

Country	Total Rice Area 1968/69 ('000 Acres)	Area of New Varieties 1966/67	Area of New Varieties 1968/69 ('000 Acres)
Burma	12,297	#	470
Ceylon	1,637	-----	17
India	91,344	2,142	6,500
Indonesia	20,950	-----	416
Laos	1,550	#	4
Malaysia (West)	1,182	104	225
Nepal	-----	-----	105
Pakistan (East)	21,212	#	300
Pakistan (West)	3,743	10	761
Philippines	7,904	204	2,592
Vietnam (South)	5,528	-----	109
TOTAL	167,347	2,460	11,499

Wheat

	Total Wheat Area 1968/69	Area of New Varieties 1966/67	Area of New Varieties 1968/69
Afghanistan	5,500	4	300
India	39,432	1,278	10,000
Iran	4,925	-----	25
Lebanon	151	-----	1
Nepal	371	16	133
Pakistan	14,977	250	6,020
Turkey	20,015	1	1,780
TOTAL	85,371	1,549	18,259

\# Less than 1,000 acres.

TABLE 2

CHANGES IN PRODUCTION OF WHEAT AND RICE FOR SELECTED ASIAN COUNTRIES 1960/61 TO 1968/69

('000 metric tons)

	1960/61 to 1964/65	1965/66	1966/67	1967/68	1968/69	% increase 1960/61-1964/65 to 1968/69
Wheat						
India	10,809	12,290	10,424	11,393	16,568	53
Pakistan	4,065	4,625	3,951	4,393	6,478	59
Total Asia	52,247	56,388	51,904	58,370	64,071	23
Total World	231,758	247,500	285,500	277,190	309,254	33
Rice						
India	53,105	46,500	45,707	59,300	59,000	11
Pakistan	16,539	17,811	16,424	19,024	19,604	19
Philippines	3,883	4,033	4,165	4,560	4,576	18
Total Asia	141,787	138,060	138,355	159,053	160,835	13
Total World	161,000	159,000	161,000	183,000	186,000	16

TABLE 3

OPERATIONAL HOLDINGS, AREA OPERATED
AND AVERAGE SIZE (BY STATE)

State	Estimated number of operational holdings ('000)	Estimated area operated ('000 acres)	Average size of an operational holding (acres)
Andhra Pradesh	3,974	28,219	7.1
Assam	1,286	4,649	3.6
Bihar	6,503	24,536	3.8
Gujarat	2,095	23,215	11.1
Jammu & Kashmir	531	1,875	3.5
Kerala	1,795	3,314	1.8
Madhya Pradesh	4,240	41,789	9.9
Madras	3,564	13,107	3.7
Maharashtra	3,570	40,975	11.5
Mysore	2,389	24,277	10.2
Orissa	2,577	12,604	4.9
Punjab	1,430	13,605	9.5
Rajasthan	2,665	36,552	13.7
Uttar Pradesh	10,579	46,978	4.4
West Bengal	3,266	12,557	3.9
Union Territories	301	1,333	4.4
India Total	50,765	329,585	6.5

TABLE 4

INTENSITY OF PRODUCTION AND POPULATION
CONCENTRATION IN INDIA AND JAPAN

	Net Agricultural Production per Hectare (US $)	Agricultural Working Population per Hectare
India	133	90
Japan	1,350	216

Notes

1. The Green Revolution, Symposium on Science and Foreign Policy, Proceedings before the Subcommittee on National Security Policy and Scientific Developments of the Committee on Foreign Affairs, House of Representatives (Washington: December 5, 1969), p. 3.

2. Ibid., pp. 29, 30.

3. See Table 1.

4. See Table 2.

5. See Table 3.

6. See Table 4.

7. Kusum Nair, The Lonely Furrow: Farming in the United States, Japan, and India (Ann Arbor: The University of Michigan Press, 1969), p. 226.

Tradition in Modern India: The Evidence of Indian Law

by

J. Duncan M. Derrett

It would be a bold man who would undertake to survey the whole of Indian law and to tell what proportion of it evidenced the persistence of tradition. The enormous bulk of legislation which is based on western models, and the apparatus of the judicial process which is admittedly derived from western techniques, owed to western inspiration, and supported by a self-conscious desire to give the public the kind of justice which Britons and Americans expect in their own homelands, all tend to support belief that Indian law is a kind of annexe (if a special kind of annexe) to the Anglo-American "common-law" consortium of legal systems. But one who reads the law reports receives a number of impressions which tell a different tale. Whether he turns his attention to the substantive law itself, or the way in which it is being administered, or in the public's and judges' attitudes towards it, he sees traces of much that is recognizably traditional. These contradictions and inconsistencies must be noticed. Different observers will utilize different segments or different aspects of the evidence in order to answer this question, and I shall give below only the gist of what has occurred to me in the course of my own experience. To sum up what I shall explain more fully in my conclusion: one can easily be deceived by appearances, and even that liability to be deceived is a traditional situation. Needless to say, no one is likely to make a useful contribution unless he is able to see below the surface of the Indian materials, and to estimate the remarks of Indians (who can be remarkably persuasive) in terms of traditionally Indian habits of self-expression.

The Public's Attitude towards Law

It can hardly be doubted but that Indians as a whole view litigation in an ambiguous way. It can be used to obtain the righting of genuine grievances; but it can be used, and frequently is used, in order to harass opponents.[1] Moreover, in the actual pursuance of litigation false pleas, false evidence and forgery are commonplace. The explanation made as early as 1837 for the extraordinary plethora of complex fabricated cases in India[2] is not only valid still, but is still the best explanation: sworn evidence is not believed by judges unless corroborated by circumstantial evidence (very few witnesses being entitled to credit), and therefore false circumstances are created or fabricated. It is normal for Indian judges, confronted by direct conflicts of evidence, to be precluded from any realistic apprehension of the true facts or the real issues in the litigation, and to have to proceed upon a notional or fictional appreciation of the facts, and to indulge in the curiosity known as "obiteration," by which the court having somehow come to a decision on the facts goes on to state what the law would have been had the facts been otherwise--in the hope that even if it has been thoroughly deceived the same result would have been achieved. Extremely lengthy judgments result[3] such as would be rare in other jurisdictions, and which, perhaps, India, with her enormous arrears of cases on the file, cannot afford.

False cases can be amazing as well as pathetic. An adoption is foisted upon a blind man and a false photograph purporting to record the ceremony is produced as proof.[4] In a crazy case in Orissa a man denied the identity of his own mother, because he wanted to prevent her alienating her share of family property to his brother.[5] In an amazing case in Bengal a leading radiologist was accused by one of his daughters of actually raping another--and was acquitted (it was an episode in a quarrel between him and his wife in which he ultimately failed to divorce her).[6] The notion that it is the lawyer's task to fabricate circumstances and produce witnesses and documents for anything is widespread and is echoed solemnly by a well-known novelist in a recent novel.[7] Lies and forgeries in court are regarded as normal, and cast little or no reflection upon the character of the participants. An amendment of the Criminal Procedure Code to enable summary conviction of such offenders to take place[8] gets little use. Litigation is a game, a drama, partaking to a very small extent of reality. It is not even a facet of reality; a mere means to other ends. Small wonder that law reform is half-hearted and consideration of the substantive law on its merits is fitful. That a marvellously small number of convicted criminals ever go to gaol, and that a marvellously high proportion of civil judgments are ultimately overturned on appeal is

notorious, but is accepted with that unique combination of
indignation and humor which is traditionally Indian.[9]

The Judiciary and Their Function

The judiciary are apt to hide behind the concept of stare
decisis, in other words to pretend that they are bound by
precedent and can do nothing without it: but this is manifestly
false, since wherever the motive for change is strong enough
ways and means can be found for by-passing older authorities,
for distinguishing, and even for overruling them. Bold judges
and benches have often done this, and they can do it the more
readily for the knowledge that apart from the Bar the greater
part of the public will neither know nor comprehend what they
are doing. However, granted that complete freedom of movement is denied them, certain striking trends can be seen.

A remarkable lack of flexibility is a characteristic of the
Indian judiciary. This is basically because of their practicing
an arcane mystery, which is divorced from the consciousness
and desires of the public to which they belong. They are rigid,
on the whole, because they have learned their craft as one learns
computer programming. It is a useful technique, but it has only
a remote connection with life. Thus to the natural conservatism
of lawyers is added the heavy disadvantage of practicing an
unreal mystery. Two examples of the inflexibility of the judiciary
would suffice. In one, inheritance was denied to a uterine half-
brother.[10] These were Hindus and the mutual relationship of
sons of one mother by different fathers is so clear, and is
recognized so plainly in the Hindu Succession Act of 1956 that
one would suppose that mutual inheritance would be recognized
on the basis of evident propriety: but because ancient texts
(wrongly) omitted to notice this relationship, and because an
old judicial authority refused, unimaginatively, to go beyond
the texts, a court could be found even in recent years to deny
that one half-brother could be heir to another. My second
example[11] is of an attempted transfer of an orchard by a Muslim
male to his daughter-in-law. He failed to put her in possession
of the income from it and died while he was attempting to have
ownership of it transferred to her name in the revenue records.
His heirs thereupon disputed the validity of the gift and the court,
with an incredible adherence to past precedents' suggestions

(for there was no case precisely in point), refused, though with manifest regret in the case of one Hindu judge, to allow that the orchard belonged to the ostensible donee. If the regret was genuine the means should have been found whereby the law could have been developed. Claims that Muslim law is being developed are often made, but the change is slow and, to some eyes, almost indiscernible.

Notwithstanding the inflexibility of the judiciary, their lack of imagination, and pedestrian adherence to older authorities,[12] their lack of confidence in themselves (possibly due to their having lived for long under the system of promotion from one cadre to another and from the High Courts to the Supreme Court, which makes them reluctant to fail to follow precedents and even more reluctant to show originality and independence), and their refusal to penalize the litigant for his vexatious and false pleading and abuse of the process of the court (note that common barratry is not a crime in India)--notwithstanding all this, there are aspects of the judicial function which are startlingly real and true to form. These are their complete aptness to show compassion to the wretched litigants before them, and their unfailing skill in balancing conflicting interests when it is their ultimate responsibility to harmonize, rather than to choose as between winner and loser.

Hardly any country can show such a record of patience with evil-minded, incompetent, dishonest, and footling litigants and their cunning legal advisers. We may take the one, but significant, aspect of matrimonial litigation which emerges when it is alleged that the petitioner has forfeited the court's protection due to unreasonable delay in presenting the petition. In one case[13] the petitioner, who claimed that her marriage was voidable for her husband's impotence, had delayed a great many years until she had exhausted the advantage which her marriage had brought herself and her relatives, and then she petitioned for nullity. The court opined that the delay was to be condoned under Indian conditions. These are conditions favorable to certain classes, normally "females," who can take advantage of what would elsewhere be regarded as dishonesty, but which in India figures as incompetence, and thus suitable for compassionate treatment. In another case[14] the wife's inordinate delay in suing for divorce on the ground that her husband had taken a concubine, with whom he was still living some fifteen years or more after the wife had left him, was excused on the ground that the court will take judicial notice of the poverty and apathy of women (though there was no evidence led as to the petitioner's apathy or poverty).

Another especially notable Indian skill is that of balancing interests, not so as to resolve the conflict, but so as to keep the status quo, leaving the contestants fit to fight another day, and without bringing them to any permanent or constructive concessions. In a case construing the Hindu Women's Rights to Property Act (1937) the Madras High Court discovered, as late as 1965, that no widow, claiming the widely-hated rights as a sharer along with her husband's male co-owners of family property, could ultimately take more than half that estate.[15] The argumentation by which that result was reached was tortuous enough, but the result was what mattered and it must have been of great satisfaction to the males of the numerous joint families of South India. In the law relating to caste it is a fact that caste tribunals can outcaste an individual (in most parts of India) and communicate the sentence to all members of the caste. In revenge the temporarily unsuccessful member may attempt to prosecute his "enemies" for defamation. The courts of today profess to have no real regard for the system of caste discipline (which runs counter to their own, and which may or may not be more genuine as a source of social authority) and there is lip-service to the idea that castes must realize that they are an anachronism and watch their steps. But the excommunicated man nevertheless fails in his prosecution, and the caste escapes unscathed, except for the costs of litigation--which are perhaps heavy enough to satisfy the disappointed complainant.[16]

When Madras passed a statute throwing open Hindu public temples to all Hindus a particular community contended that it was not a public temple, and then that, if it was, the statute contravened its right to manage its own affairs within the scope of the freedom of religion guaranteed by the Constitution. The Supreme Court held[17] in a consummate piece of juridical ingenuity that the untouchables who had now been permitted to enter, for the first time, the temple of a Brahman Hindu sect (which was held to be a public temple) had not been permitted to interfere with the worship of the deity, and therefore might not approach the idol any nearer than might any Hindu other than the actual ministrants. A further example is the famous

Excommunication Case[18] which, though it appeals to me, has
been uniformly condemned in India. A Bombay statute prohibited
excommunication, and a member of a Muslim sect who was in confrontation with the head of that sect, and had been excommunicated by
him, desired to have his excommunication declared null and void.
The Supreme Court found that the freedom of a religious sect to
manage its own affairs would be infringed (contrary to the
Constitution) if all excommunications could be rendered void,
including excommunications based upon breach of a religious
rule: thus excommunication on religious grounds could not be
tampered with on the basis of any statute. Public antipathy
to the decision is based, I surmise, upon the supposition that
excommunications are based upon intrigue, faction, or the
corrupt exercise of autocratic power: but surely the Supreme
Court was wise enough to see that no such thing could be pre-
sumed, that if such _were_ the case the aggrieved would be able
to prove that the excommunication was not _bona_ _fide_, and that
if a religious sect could not control its members by the exercise
of a spiritual sanction there would be an end to the constitutional
protection of religion, which is one of the cornerstones of the
so-called secular state that is India. Apart from this case the
courts show themselves admirably equipped to cope with disputes
between religious sects, which tend to bedevil Indian life even
after Independence, and have proved to be a most useful check
upon the rather hasty and ill-advised acts of the executive.[19]

The notorious Cow-Slaughter Cases[20] provide an outstanding
instance of the court's skill at balancing, without reconciling,
opposed interests. The Constitution, somewhat hypocritically,[21]
envisages the prohibition of cow-slaughter. It is known that the
objections to the slaughter of bovine cattle are superstitious, not
practical; and consequently where statutes purported to prohibit
totally the slaughter of buffaloes, bulls, calves, and cows,
irrespective of their age or usefulness, the Supreme Court were
able to hold, at the suit of hide-dealers and gut-dealers (who are
naturally Muslims), that this was an unconstitutional interference
with the fundamental right to practice a trade or profession.[22]
The total ban on slaughter was against the country's economic
interests and therefore unreasonable. A more realistic decision
it would have been hard to find, except for the curious qualifica-
tion, which mars the judgment: all _cows_ are exempt from
slaughter, whatever their age or usefulness. Now Hindu writers,
attacking the Supreme Court's decisions, urge that total ban on

slaughter of bovine cattle and buffaloes should be held good,
since it is known that Hindus (the majority) strongly object to
such slaughter.[23] It is assumed as a matter of course that
Muslim hide-dealers or gut-dealers, whose trade would be
affected by their having to wait for the natural deaths of the
cattle in question, could change their trade and take up another.
In any other country, I suggest, the decision of the constitution-
ality of such a ban would be determined on the basis of the
nation's needs. But in the last case in the series the basic
assumption was that the Muslim dealers have as much right to
their hereditary occupation and the means of pursuing it as the
cow-lovers have to try to prevent the slaughter of their favorites.
In a society dominated still by the idea of caste such an outlook
is understandable.

A further example of balancing interests is the subtle ruling
that though a charity may be a charity in the eyes of a Muslim
it is not necessarily a charity in terms of the revenue law and
so exempt from tax, or entitled to the court's protection as a
trust.[24]

The Substantive Law Itself

It would be possible to take up many pages dividing the
statute law of India into three categories: laws foreign to India
and her traditions and hostile to the outlook of her people;[25]
laws fully compatible with her tradition and ethics;[26] and laws
irrelevant to that tradition.[27] A full discussion would be out of
place, and indeed very hard to achieve. Where tradition can be
best assessed is surely in the progress of that part of the Indian
law which professed in the last few decades to be based on the
past, on Indian indigenous legal tradition. The failure to reform
Muslim and Christian laws relating to marriage and inheritance
is not due to a lack of skill, but a lack of courage, accompanied
by a desire not to arouse unnecessary antagonism in the communities in question. The Hindu Marriage Act, 1955, fails to provide
divorce for adultery or cruelty: this is in striking contrast to the
Special Marriage Act, 1954, and must be based on respect for
Hindu tradition, which would be threatened by the possibility of
"hotel bedroom" divorce cases, and false cruelty cases. As it
is, pleas by wives that their husbands "mercilessly beat them,
deprived them of their ornaments, and drove them out of the

house" are common form pleading. The revolutionary descent
and distribution provisions of the Hindu Succession Act, 1956,
are commented upon effectively by the Madhya Pradesh Land
Revenue statute of not long afterwards[28] which turned the clock
back so far as the most important category of property, tenures
in agricultural land, were concerned: the fact that a few years
later the state resiled from this might be urged as a reinforce-
ment of reforming notions[29] but the large amount of case-law
attempting to take agricultural land altogether out of the central
statute's scope[30] shows that tradition is very much alive in that
quarter. The Special Marriage Act itself has been radically
de-codified by a most curious statute tending to validate marriages,
even between Hindus, though the spouses are within the prohibited
degrees set out in the Act, if custom would have enabled them to
marry had they married under their traditional, personal law.[31]

The Concept of Traditionality

Notwithstanding the apparent gross novelties in the
Constitution, with its freedom, equality, and liberty--concepts
foreign, as they sound, to Indian tradition, even to Indian
tradition in its modified, Anglo-Indian form, a persistent effort
is being made to believe, and to encourage the belief, that
the Indian Constitution and the general principles of Indian law
are based on Indian indigenous ideas and traditions. Important
examples of this are the colloquium held at Madras,[32] a
conference held at Patna,[33] and another conference held at
Poona[34]--all directed to these ends. B. N. Rau, when speaking
even of his preliminary work on the Constitution, stressed that
some principles from Kauṭilya's Arthaśāstra were consonant
with this work. An attempt to see Indian judicial decisions as
viable in terms of Sanskritic norms is often to be seen.[35] An
ex-Chief Justice of two Indian High Courts writes solemnly,
and persuasively, of the need to reform the penal law of India
so as to conform to a text of a well-known Sanskrit jurist, who
evidently foresaw difficulties which the Anglo-Indian jurists did
not.[36] No persistent reader of the lesser Indian juridical
periodicals can fail to be struck with the continual flow of
articles on the ancient Indian judicial system. The intended
comparison is surely motivated by a desire to see the current
system as in some real fashion related or capable of being
related to the pre-British. Marc Galanter is certainly right in
suggesting[37] that no one seriously wishes to return, legislatively,
to the pre-British method of administering justice: but that does not

mean that a belief in the essential rightness of the old ideas is
not an actual, and perhaps important part of the background, if
not the foreground, of modern Indian law.

The Desire for Continuity

Apart from a famous case on the nature of "Hinduness,"
which quite naturally relies upon traditional sources (and
markedly ignores Anglo-Indian case-law)[38] we can find examples of Indian judges seeking to see the Anglo-Indian law which
they propound as foreshadowed, and to that extent justified, in
purely traditional terms. How successful they are depends
upon their knowledge and skill in traditional materials (which, I
may say, leaves something still to be desired--as is not
surprising).[39] But instances must be pointed out where the law
stated purports to be traditional in justification[40] or the judge
says happily that the ancient law and the modern coincide, and
he is the better staisfied for that.[41] There are plenty of instances
where the judges say that a new age has dawned and that traditional notions based on custom or the dharmaśāstra are not
viable in court-law any more,[42] or that textual, traditional law
must be 'liberally' construed to further the interests of society.[43]
No regret is shown, and the confidence of the current system is
unshaken by appeals to traditional notions. But this, I suggest,
is because of law's self-conscious rôle as a norm: and to this
I must return below.

The Traditional Attitude to Law

The inherent contradictions, and other puzzling features in
this picture, cannot (I submit) be understood without a knowledge
of how law worked before the British period.[44] It is idle, I
suggest, to argue that after all the Anglo-Indian system has been
in use for two centuries and the public have become fully adjusted
to it. They have become adjusted to it in the sense that one
becomes adjusted to using an escalator--it does not supersede
the staircase. The traditional ideas continue to circulate in
some segments of the population which are still not reached by
material in English, and which have always been attentive to
the Sanskrit epics and their regional versions, to the purāṇas
and to purely indigenous normative religious and ethical literature. These pervasive notions, which cut right across Anglo-
Indian standards, form the concrete layers upon which the

mental structures of most Indians are built up, and however
fanciful and "with-it" those structures may be, and however
well they may deceive the casual observer, it is upon the
foundation that the whole stands, and actual behavior, in the
last resort, depends upon it.

The traditional rôle of the dharmaśāstra was not one of
setting out the rules of law which would invariably be applied
by royal tribunals. Its rôle was more complex, more subtle,
and ultimately more effective.[45] It was a social norm-making
medium applying a suction to all elements of Indian society
(other than non-Hindu or non-Hinduizing society) which had not
reached pure Brahmanical customs. Justice and prestige were
indissolubly linked in it. But the actual administration of
justice worked upon another line, that of expediency. Mr. Justice
Gajendragadkar (as he then was) performed a valuable service
when he pointed out that in the ancient system the principles of
arthaśāstra were to be taken account of by the legal adviser, the
judge's assessor, as well as those of dharmaśāstra.[46] The
classical studies of Kane and Varadachariar not unnaturally tend
to ignore this, because they were intended to show the British
(amongst others) that there was a viable book-law of a purely
indigenous description before the British came to India. The
mistake the British made[47] was to believe their Bengali advisers
and to utilize for administration of law solely the dharmaśāstra
texts, naturally (at first) in English translation only, with all
the risks that involved. What really happened prior to their time?

I want to call your attention to two inscriptions. One belongs
to the sixteenth century and has been used only for a purpose
differing very much from mine.[48] The other belongs to the
twelfth century and has not been used before.[49] In the first
a most important legal point was established, namely that a
matha should descend to the heirs of the body of the holder,
being qualified in spiritual as well as hereditary respects, by
primogeniture to the eldest in learning as well as birth. In the
second the social status, and exclusive functions, and rights of
the caste or group of castes called Rathakāras were established
beyond dispute. The problems had been referred to appropriate
authorities[50] and those authorities' signatures, or the equivalent,
appear in the documents. The qualifications of the authors of
these decisions are evidently that they are completely dissociated,
not from the practical effects of the decisions, but from the

social, political, or economic contest which led ultimately to
the formulation of the problem, which was equally real, requiring
these deliberate and expensive responses, whether approached
as a genuine legal conflict or an administrative quandary. The
signatures which seem to carry most weight are of Bhaṭṭas and
Somayājīs, men who are evidently prominent Brahmans, dis-
tinguished for their caste observances and spiritual functions.
The importance of the inscriptions lies particularly in their
actually citing and quoting the literary sources upon which those
referees purported to rely for their decision. From these it
is evident that the dharmaśāstra was used, but not in isolation
from religious, sectarian (e. g. , Pañcarātra), and (in the second
case) technical traditional literature.

Thus to arrive at a decision binding upon Hindu society
recourse must be made to expediency, custom, the actual
norms overtly accepted by the people, and to which they had
specifically to be recalled, and the spiritual and normative
sources where these are regarded as relevant in the light of
the instant controversy. The background was no doubt intrigue,
jealousy, faction, self-seeking: the decision is arrived at
in the light of what is politic, and is expressed in terms of what
is righteous and traditional.

The Real and the Unreal

We are now in a position to revert to our commencement.
Judges are experts in the technique of judicial administration,
a highly skilled technical performance. Its contact with reality
is partial, but in those parts it is real. The litigants, particularly
in family law, are ruthless operators, intending to bend the
judicial process to their personal ends: they do not believe that
the system actually gives justice in the sense of righteousness;
they want to persuade the "royal" power to intervene in their
favor and to win a temporary advantage over their opponents by
any means. The judges attempt to provide a solution which
would not be unjust even if the successful plaintiff had put up a
false case. No one believes that the apparently judicial solution
is better, intrinsically, than an administrative expedient to give
temporary relief to the warring parties. The really righteous
answer could come only from judges of special qualifications
having a full intuitive knowledge of the real issues: and this,

almost by definition, the Anglo-Indian judicial system is not
designed to supply. Litigation is an adventure into the unreal
in order to obtain artha (temporal advantage) the actual
employment of which in conjunction with dharma (righteousness)
and kāma (pleasure) it is the individual's task to determine.

Meanwhile the judiciary exercise the "king's" prerogative
in balancing conflicting interests, without determining their
actual merits. This is a recognizably traditional function. And
the law is an educative norm, in that the "king's" court
administers as a latter-day vyavahāra predetermined norms,
which the learned pretend are a new smṛti (a "manufactured"
tradition!),[51] which the public must accept as their judicial
ideal, within which they must operate in terms of law, whatever
their level of advancement in terms of righteousness. In due
course it is supposed the new smṛti will draw all customs to
itself.[52] The fact that individual judges may not believe in it
personally is neither here nor there. The professors of
dharmaśāstra accepted that the provisions of the śāstra were
collectively "just," though they did not personally believe in
or approve of them individually. It was not their business to
approve of them, but to know them and to teach them!

There is a lesson in all this for the foreign intervenor. To
teach Indians company law, international law, constitutional
law and the like as part of the administrative technique makes
perfect sense. But one who would teach law as something which
India needs; one who would tell Indians how they should frame
their statute laws or "improve" their judicial system must, if
he hopes for success, possess the qualities which the old referees
had. He must be free from those faults which, in Indian eyes,
disqualify a person from teaching others. We know very well
that teaching, in universities, goes on at the hands of people who
do not have these qualities; but it is not teaching: it is a pretense
of doing so. Small wonder that the teachers are not listened to.
The man capable of conferring anything on India and Indians must
conform to the śloka of Manu (X.63):--

> ahiṃsā satyam asteyam śaucam indriya-nigrahaḥ
> etam sāmāsikam dharmam cāturvarṇye 'bravīn Manuḥ.

"Abstension from injury, truth, abstension from misappropri-
ation, purity (i.e., abhorrence of defilement), and restraint of
the senses (i.e., not being ruled by them): that is the epitome of
righteousness which Manu declared for all four varṇas."

Notes

1. Sreethava v. Jawala [1970] Ker. L.R. 148, 155 (litigation as blackmail).

2. A Penal Code Prepared by the Indian Law Commissioners (Calcutta, 1837), Notes, pp. 41ff. (Note G.).

3. A good example is Mahendra v. Sushila A.I.R. 1965 S.C. 364. This is reproduced at pp. 652ff. of my Course, Problems in South Asian Private Law (1970) available from The Librarian, University of Michigan Law School, Ann Arbor, Michigan.

4. Govinda v. Chimabai A.I.R. 1968 Mys. 309. On lies in adoption cases see N. Das at A.I.R. 1965 Journ. 27, 29b.

5. Purna Chandra v. Chandramani A.I.R. 1966 Or. 98. She was not a low caste woman whom his father had picked up.

6. Sachindranath v. Nilima (1969) 74 Cal. W.N. 168 or A.I.R. 1970 Cal. 38. An incomplete copy of this appears at Problems (above, n.2), pp. 386ff.

7. R.K. Narayan, The Vendor of Sweets (New York, Viking, 1967), p. 179. A judicial animadversion to the same effect (deserving of attention) appears at Mahendra (above, n.2) at p. 404b (Problems, p. 692). See also Charles Morrison, "Munshi's and their Masters" (Jan. 1971: mimeographed) on the lawyer's clerk/tout and their clientele.

8. Sec. 479A, introduced by Act 26 of 1955.

9. V.D. Mahajan, Chief Justice Gajendragadkar... (Delhi, etc., 1966) at various places in the judge's speeches.

10. Ghusly v. Bhorriya 1959 M.P.L.J. 62, following Ekoba v. Kashiram A.I.R. 1922 Bom. 27 in spite of the outlook certified by the Hindu Succession Act, 1956.

11. Noor Jahan Begam v. Muftkhar A.I.R. 1970 All. 170. See especially paragraph 50.

12. I must in fairness draw attention to Justice V.R. Krishna Iyer's well meant, but vain attempt to hold that a Muslim had no right to multiple matrimony, at Shahulameedu v. Subaida [1970] Ker. L.T. 4, which illustrates as much the optimism of the judge as the futility of the approach he adopted. The same judge animadverted, in K.P. Khader v. K.K.P. Kunhamina [1970] Ker. L.T. 237, on the 'antiquated' Muslim rule inhibiting the gift of undivided shares (musha).

13. S. v. R. A.I.R. 1968 Del. 79. Derrett, Critique of Modern Hindu Law (Bombay, Tripathi, 1970), paragraph 401. Problems, pp. 325ff.

14. Bannubai v. Ratna [1966] Jubb. L.J. 690. Cf. Smt. Nirmoo v. Nikka A.I.R. 1968 Del. 260; Lalithamma v. Kannan A.I.R. 1966 Mys. 178.

15. Manicka v. Arunachala [1964] 2 Mad. L.J. 519 F.B. (Problems, pp. 271ff.).

16. S. Varadiah Chetty v. P. Parthasarathy 1964 2 Mad. L.J. 433 (Derrett, Religion, Law and the State in India, London, 1968, pp. 472-3), followed in S. Appa Rao v. Deenabandhu (1969) 35 Cuttack L.T. cvii (No. 179).

17. Sri Venkataramana Devaru v. State of Mysore (1958) 21 Sup. C.J. 382 (Religion, Law and the State, cited in last note, pp. 468-9).

18. Sardar Syedna v. Tyebbhai A.I.R. 1962 S.C. 853 (Religion, Law and the State, pp. 474-5, 478, 481).

19. Tejraj v. State of M.B. A.I.R. 1958 M.P. 115 (Problems, pp. 40ff.). But M. Ghouse's criticism (at J. Ind. L. Inst. 10, 1968, 521-7) of Azeez Basha v. Union of India A.I.R. 1968 S.C. 662 (a case where a 'minority's' University was reorganized by Parliament), on the basis that form was consulted more than substance, seems sound.

20. M.H. Quareshi v. State of Bihar A.I.R. 1958 S.C. 731; A.H. Quraishi v. State A.I.R. 1961 S.C. 448; Mohd. Faruk v. State of M.P. A.I.R. 1969 N.S.C. 14.

21. Art. 48: "The State shall endeavor to organise agriculture and animal husbandry on modern and scientific lines and shall, in particular, take steps for preserving and improving the breeds, and prohibiting the slaughter, of cows and calves and other milch and draught cattle." The words "and prohibiting the slaughter" are slipped in, as it were, as if subordinate to the words preceding them--but the orthodox elements in the Constituent Assembly regarded them as the substantive provisions.

22. Constitution, Art. 19: "(1) All citizens shall have the right-- ... (g) to practise any profession, or to carry on any occupation, trade or business..., (6) Nothing in sub-clause (g) of the said clause shall affect the operation of any existing law in so far as it imposes, or prevent the State from making any law imposing, in the interests of the general public, reasonable restrictions on the exercise of the right conferred by the said clause..."

23. P.C. Jain at 1 Allahabad L Rev. 129-136 (1969). See also V.K.S. Chaudhary at A.I.R. 1962 Journ. 25-7.

24. For the subject see Fazlul Rabbi v. State of W. Bengal A.I.R. 1965 S.C. 1722 (Critique, paragraph 500), and compare Meer Mahomed Israil Khan v. Sashti Churn I.L.R. 19 Cal. 412 (1892).

25. E.g. Income Tax Act, 1922; Central Sales Tax Act, 1956; Prevention of Corruption Act, 1947; Representation of the People Act, 1951; Coal Bearing Areas (Acquisition and Development) Act, 1957; and perhaps also the Preventive Detention Act, 1950 and the Unlawful Activities (Prevention) Act, 1967.

26. E.g. the following Acts: Fatal Accidents (1855), Workmen's Compensation (1923), Minimum Wages (1948), Coal Miners Provident Fund (1948), Factories (1948), Employee's Provident Fund (1952), Industrial Disputes (1947), Payment of Bonus (1965), Essential Commodities (1955).

27. E.g. Contract Act, 1872; Insolvency Acts, 1909, 1920; Insurance Act, 1912; Copyright Act, 1914; Carriage of Goods by Sea Act, 1925; Partnership Act, 1932; Motor

Vehicles Acts, 1913-1939; All India Services Acts, 1951, 1963; and all the many University statutes.

28. Madhya Pradesh Land Revenue Code, 1959; see sec. 64.

29. The same, amended and reenacted in 1961.

30. E.g. Prema Devi v. Jt. Dir. of Consol. 1969 Allahabad L.J. 253; also Ramlali v. Bhagunti A.I.R. 1968 M.P. 247 (Problems, pp. 734a).

31. Special Marriage (Amendment) Act, 32 of 1963.

32. Bull. Inst. Trad. Culture (Madras), 2 (1964), 195-234.

33. March, 1969.

34. Seminar on Comparative Evaluation of Modern Political Theories and Rajaniti, Poona, June 1970: "Working Paper" (with that title) distributed by the Executive Chairman, V.V. Deshpande.

35. Peramanayakam v. Sivaraman A.I.R. 1952 Mad. 419 (Problems, pp. 567ff.), at pp. 471ff. (per Panchapakesa Ayyar, J.).

36. R.L. Narasimham at J. Ind. L. Inst. 11 (1969), 321-7.

37. Lecture at the Spring 1969 meeting of The Association for Asian Studies, Boston, Mass.

38. Shastri Yagnapurushdasji v. Muldas A.I.R. 1966 S.C. 1119 (Problems, pp. 834ff.; Religion, Law and the State, pp. 47-51)

39. Shamlal v. Amar Nath A.I.R. 1970 S.C. 1643 and Raman Nadar v. Snehappoo Rasalamma A.I.R. 1970 S.C. 1759 are both unfortunate examples of the Supreme Court (and its Bar) knowing less of Indian (Hindu) legal history than they should.

40. Outstanding cases are those which interpret Parliament's intention, with regard to adoption, as expressed at sec. 12 of the Hindu Adoptions and Maintenance Act, 1956, so as, not to avoid 'relation back' (of the adoption) (the inconvenience

of which is dramatically illustrated at, e.g., Eramma v.
Muddappa A.I.R. 1966 S.C. 1137), but to underpin it:
Sawan Ram v. Kalawanti A.I.R. 1967 S.C. 1761 and Sita
Bai v. Ramchandra A.I.R. 1970 S.C. 343, the literature
on which is given at my study of these cases in Critique,
paragraphs 179ff. Sawan Ram is at Problems, pp. 450ff.

41. Saminatha v. Vageesan I.L.R. [1940] Mad. at p. 108,
     per Patanjali Sastri, J.

42. Critique, paragraph 507 n.2 (pp. 396-7). Rama Ananda v.
     Appa 70 Bom. L.R. 773 (1968) (Problems, pp. 751ff.),
     praised by K.C. Srivastava at Indian Advocate 9 (1969),
     100ff. The Constitution has cut down some old customs,
     e.g. hereditary priestly monopolies: Baijnath v. Ramnath
     A.I.R. 1951 H.P. 32; G. Birahari v. Thinganam A.I.R.
     1960 Man. 34. The Anglo-Hindu legal outlook may affront
     tradition: Tiruvenkatachariar v. Andalamma [1969]
     1 Andhra W.R. 142 F.B. (Problems, pp. 54ff., Critique,
     App. I. Chandrasekhara v. Kulandaivelu A.I.R. 1963
     S.C. 185 (Problems, pp. 163ff.) incidentally negatives
     customary standards which the Anglo-Hindu law had ignored.
     Moreover   adition was briskly ruled out in Gedela Sanyasi v.
     State C.R. 279 of 1967 rep. at 1969 Cuttack L.T. cxxxvi
     (no. 215) (a husband cannot be convicted for his wife's
     offences). In Sumil v. Satirani A.I.R. 1969 Cal. 573
     patriarchal notions of the Hindu family were abandoned in
     the interests of a child's welfare (a guardianship matter).

43. The dissenting judgment of Hedge, J., in V.D. Dhanwatey
     v. Commr. of I.T. A.I.R. 1968 S.C. 683, paragraph 31
     (p. 696). The same judge had his way with the subject
     matter two years later.

44. Derrett, "The concept of law according to Medhatithi,"
     in W. Hoenerbach, ed., Der Orient in der Forschung
     (Festschrift O. Spies), Wiesbaden, 1967, 18ff. Also the
     early chapters in Religion, Law and the State in India
     (1968), cited above.

45. The best treatment is that of R. Lingat, Les Sources du
     droit..., an English translation of which, under the title
     The Classical Law of India, has been advertised by the
     University of California Press.

46. P.B. Gajendragadkar at A.I.R. 1963 Journ. 18-26.

47. Derrett, "The Indian Subcontinent under European Influence" at J. Gilissen, ed., Bibliographical Introduction to Legal History and Ethnology, E/8 (Brussels, 1969).

48. Annual Rep. of S. Ind. Epigraphy, 1936-7, No. 135, pp. 91ff., sec. 79. T.V. Mahalingam, J. Or. Res. (Madras), 25 (1957), 78-9. Religion, Law and the State, p. 168n.

49. Ann. Rep. of Epig. No. 558 of 1904 = No. 603 of S. Ind. Inscriptions XVII (1964).

50. I have discussed who these are in the first inscription at the P.B. Desai Felicitation Volume (to appear).

51. S. Radhakrishnan at the Foreword to P.H. Valavalkar's Hindu Social Institutions (Bombay, 1939).

52. Those of us who are acquainted with India are aware that Hindus (but not Muslims, contemporary Parsis, or Christians) see no incongruity whatever in a person being at one and the same time a "social reformer" and a leading prestige-figure in his group (cf., the story of Marie Stopes).

The Indian Novel Written in English--A Mirror of India?

by

Margaret E. Derrett

In 1952 my first child, a daughter, was born in Poona. It was my first visit to India. I had been attending the School of Oriental and African Studies in London to learn Marathi and my teacher had provided not only linguistic training, but also an orientation course including practical instruction on how to wear a sari and to eat an Indian meal. My husband too had done his best to prepare me, and yet the East was a shock, and adjustment to it hard, even though the predisposition to adjust was certainly there. We had gone to learn more about India and her inhabitants, but when I came away, I felt, despite genuine efforts on the part of my Indian women friends, that what I knew about their domestic life was very limited; and I was tantalized. They were only too willing to illustrate the cooking of a particular dish (not of course in their kitchen) and to hold a seven month dinner for which I was told to buy an auspiciously colored sari. I even talked to excited women in Purdah in the backward district of Etawah (U. P.). They exclaimed and lamented over the meanness of those who had given me only two rings; but this, I knew, was only the bare frame of the picture.

In the larger cities of Bombay and Delhi which we visited we had friends who spoke perfect English. They told us, and showed us, all we wanted to know about their households. Our dear friend Mrs. Kamala Dongerkery of Bombay, a woman of charm and intelligence (now author of fine books on Indian embroidery, Indian jewelry, Indian toys, and an autobiography, On Wings of Time (1968)) told me indeed of her marriage at the age of eleven, but the public nature of her work and the international circle in which she moved indicated that she was no ordinary Indian woman. I heard that two Indian women had written in detail about their lives and was able to find Laksmibai

Tilak's autobiography called I Follow After published in 1950
and Venu Chitale's In Transit, and through these books I really
felt I was able to learn more. The quality of the English appeared
to me slightly quaint, but that was not what interested me; it was
the content and the sincerity with which they were written.

My approach since then continues to be that of an average
Englishwoman interested in India and Indians; not a literary
critic but someone interested in the content of the works (particularly in relation to their authors), and to their authors, as a
group of Indians, in relation to their society. Those two Indian
women had been induced to record their lives in factual detail
no doubt at the instigation of (and certainly for the pleasure of)
European and American residents in India and because they were
aware of some of the differences between their readers and
themselves, and the rapidity of change within their society.
Similar books are still written in English or translated, and I
would consider some of them to be a mirror of India which does
not distort, useful for those who are not able to go to study there
with thorough knowledge of a relevant vernacular; and for those
who have not the good fortune to be accepted for a considerable
time in an Indian household. They are not intended by their
authors to be what our novelists would call a novel. In his
preface to Marali Mannige by K. S. Karanth, translated from
the Kannaḍa in 1950 by A. N. Murthy Rao, the author writes
"I have tried to picture in this book the life and struggles of
three generations of my people who inhabited the ever beautiful
strip of land on the West Coast of India...to me it is not my
literary achievement that is so important as the hard struggle
of my ancestors to whom I owe my very existence." In the
Journal of Asian Studies, Vol. 28, No. 4 (August 1969), I found
a review of one such book by Edward Dimock of Chicago, A House
Full of People by Romen Basu (1968). It ends as follows:

> If it does not quite come off as a novel, the book succeeds
> in other ways. It shows in a way that scholarly studies
> could never achieve the problems of people from a past-
> oriented society in the modern world. It shows in a
> touching way the tribulations and some of the comforts of
> that now awkward but still sadly dignified institution, the
> extended family. It is not a book which I read with great
> aesthetic delight, nor is it a book which I would recommend,
> except to those with small experience of Indian society,
> for information. But when a modern Indian writes with

sensitivity about his own culture, especially of its
current throes, those who seek to understand that
culture would be wise to listen.

It seems to me that what Mr. Dimock criticizes is the
extent to which such writing claims to be literature and the
extent to which its author tries to inform the reader unacquainted
with India of factual details that will help him, but will merely
irritate an Indian or an Indian specialist. These are thorns that
grow in this field. What very often is approved as a novel of
literary merit has passed some test by Western standards which
may not be the ultimate one. And it is a fact that Indians most
highly trained in Western literary standards e.g., Balachandra
Rajan (scholar and author of The Dark Dancer (1958) and the
aptly entitled Too Long in the West (1961)) may fail, ironically
enough, on that very account. The second criticism depends
upon the readership of these novels. As David McCutchion says
in his Introduction to Indian Writing in English (1968) (p. 17),

> So far as I know, little attempt has been made to define
> and analyse the Indian readership of Indian writing in
> English, yet there can be no clear understanding of
> this literature without an understanding of this group--
> the pressures upon it, its idea of itself, and its relations
> with the rest of India. It is on these conditions rather
> than on the specific issue of language that will depend the
> possibility of a really great writer emerging among
> Indians who write in English--genius can fashion its
> own tools but is fashioned by circumstances.

Research needs to be done in this field.

Various broad assumptions can reasonably be made about
the readers, namely that they are fairly intelligent middle class
folk (as R.P. Jhabvala wrote to me some years ago) but the fact
that they may live anywhere in the world and that India is markedly
different from America, Australia, or Europe (not least in climate,
flora and fauna) means that these environmental details matter to
us and that what seems over-lush description to an Indian can be
the first perception of a different milieu to a Westerner, and the
oppressive heat and its effect on all life (as also the impact of
the monsoon rains) must be conveyed. These are the conditions
of life. I agree that the descriptions in general are overdone,
and any mannered writing is accentuated in such a context: but

there has yet to be born some Tolstoy who does not need to
elaborate on the extremes of the Russian winter.

Here is a little description from Anita Desai's <u>Cry the Peacock</u>
(1963). Maya is waiting for her father in the garden (p. 31):

> He has been called in by a visitor and now I am waiting
> for him in the·shade of a bougainvillia arbour, where
> the light turns from lilac to mauve to purple, from
> peach to orange to crimson, as the small whispers of
> breeze turn and turn again the heavy load of blossoms
> upon the air. I see the sky through them, and the vast
> lawn stretching out towards the creeper-hung bungalow,
> and all the world is tinted like sweet sherbet.

I regard much of the discussion about either the literary
merits in themselves or the sociological value of these novels,
and their down-grading on either or both counts, as largely
irrelevancies compared with the authors' desire to communicate
and to put down truthfully what they know. As Nayantara Sahgal
says at p. 230 of her most recent novel, <u>Storm in Chandigarh</u>
(1969), "Is there anything on earth to compare with the great
glory of communication--and that is only possible when people
accept each other in truth?"

In this light most scholars (within India and without) welcome
translations of regional language novels provided that the
translators are equal to their task, and that they are translating
into their mother tongue and are thus aware of all its overtones.
The cultural climate changes so rapidly that, it seems to me,
translations have to be made afresh every few decades. No
non-specialist can hope to have his interest in something strange
aroused by archaic language. Novels such as <u>Godan</u> by Prem
Chand (translated by J. Ratan and P. Lal in 1957) and <u>Chemmeen</u>
by T. S. Pillai (translated by N. Menon in 1962 and also by
Gordon Roadarmel in 1968) are eagerly received inside India
and are valuable steps towards arousing general literary
appreciation and a feeling of literary unity in that vast country.
Through them we may contrast regional language literature with
writing originally conceived in English and thus be assured in
any criticism of or comment we make on the quality of the latter.

There is the question of distortion. It has been said that
Indians writing in English, probably <u>because</u> they write in English,

have more observation, irony, and subtlety. They have not
only been trained in Western literary techniques but have also,
in most cases, come to learn the language in their teens and
through western classics; and therefore the cultural auras and
expectations of the West are subconsciously present, while more
simple, basic, childish instincts are muted. The problem of
their writing in English must be related to their response to
literature in English or what they have seen of it. In The
Literary Criterion, Vol. 7, No. 3 (Winter 1966), p. 18, M. G.
Krishnamurti says, in his "Foreign Literatures and Problems
in Response,"

> The problems inherent in our responding to literature
> in English which to most of us is a second language and
> is, at best, a literary medium, seem to result from
> firstly the difficulty in having the same inwardness with
> the language that a native speaker can have, and secondly,
> the differences in cultural background and the resultant
> differences in framework.

It is all very well to belittle translations, but we must
realize that trans-Indian readership continues to be a reality
only in the English language. The role of Hindi is growing but
has not yet replaced English. Efforts by Westerners to specialize
in Indian languages and their cultures, and by Indians to cooperate
in translation ventures should gradually lead to more truthful
re-creation in translation. Sujit Mukerjee says in his essay on
Indo-English literature in Critical Essays on Indian Writing in
English (1969), "I sometimes suspect that the main reason why
Indo-English literature has not yet been taken seriously in India
or abroad is because the quality of English found in their translations is generally execrable". Unless suitable translations of
valuable literary works are produced no standard can evolve.

One might be inclined to presume that an Indian writer who is
bilingual would provide a clearer mirror of Indian life than would
translations into English of works by Indian writers originally
cast in the regional languages and so instinct with Indian atmosphere, intimate allusions, and native overtones. My problem has
been to make an estimate how far, by and large, this is true and,
as we shall see, I find it only marginally true.

Zulfikar Ghose, born in Pakistan, first a refugee to India
and now resident in England, shows us another conflict; that the

author feels the blurring of the mirror caused by his own rootlessness. He received his literary education at Keele University
in England and is the author of two novels, The Contradictions
(1966) and The Murder of Aziz Khan (1967). This is how he
describes his situation in Confessions of a Native Alien, his
autobiography, published in 1965:

> This distinction between the two countries of my early
> life has been the schizophrenic theme of much of my
> thinking. It created a psychological conflict and a
> pressing need to know that I do belong somewhere.
> Worse than meaning is language; even when there is
> no doubt about a fact, the very attempt to translate
> that fact into a verbal statement can diminish or enhance
> the precise nature of it. Nothing I can say can ever be
> true, for even when an experience is a clear unambiguous
> image in my mind I could never recreate it in a clear
> unambiguous language; language which liberates also
> impedes, literary language whose stylistic polish may
> give pleasure also distorts. Oh my people, how can I
> tell you that I woo the English language each morning
> and she divorces me each night.

Sasthi Brata, author of My God Died Young, The Autobiography
of a Modern Man without a Country (1968) was educated in an
English medium Calcutta school which he thinks landed him
between two systems of values and thought. He is now resident
in England and says that the deepest tragedy of British rule was
that it produced individuals like himself who can neither feel an
identity with their own people nor accept "the glare, the steel
muscle concept of life as it exists in America." These authors
throw light on the subject of our lecture; and in a world where
refugees of all kinds are sadly increasing, these are no isolated
cries. Their authors are compelled by inner discomforts to write.

Another approach to the problem of clear communication in
English by a writer whose second language it is is contained in
G.V. Desani's book. I will not call it a novel; he calls it a
"gesture", All About H. Hatterr. It was first published in 1951
and is about to be republished with a foreword by Alan Burgess.
Mr. Desani was living and working in London and wrote to
express himself and in a language, style, and form that can only
have given him a sense of release from what he calls "Mutual
Introduction" (p. 10):

I write rigmarole English, staining your goodly, godly
tongue maybe, but friend, I forsook my Form, School,
and Head, while you stuck to yours learning reading,
'riting and 'rithmetic ... it is not because I seek a
clown's abandon nor, I swear, the rewards of a mounte-
bank, truly; not because I crave the gain of an unmerited
prize, or wealth, or riches or honour, or more, or less;
but because by the Lord God of Hosts, the Holy who made
you of the happy breed and I of the stricken, He above
knowing the aught of making mortal things; I am lonely.'

Before passing on I should like to leave a thought with you.
How far do we encourage distortion or accept it as part of the
old myth of the romance of the East? How far do we accept new
theories with all their fascinating ramifications? I would choose
as an example the theories of Edward Shils of Chicago about
metropolitan and provincial cultures which may encourage the
East to think her future lies in imitation of Western patterns and
values but which, as a by-product, hinders us in our attempts to
see the present East clearly. Let us think of novels about India
written by Europeans and Americans (I regret I have not read
many of them, but we may take the work of John Masters for
example) and ask ourselves how far they romanticize and distort
our vision. How far do commercial pressures dictate forms and
themes?

Kamala Markandaya suggests in her novel Possession (1963)
(p. 116):

The East was too strident, too dissonant, too austere,
too raw: it had to be muted, toned down, tarted up--
its music larded with familiar rhythms, its literature
wrenched into shapes recognized by Western tradition,
its dances made palatable by an infusion of known idioms,
its people taught to genuflect before understatement before
a measure of acceptance came. Undilute East always
came lapdog fashion to the West; mutely asking to be not
too little and not too much but just right.

Ruth P. Jhabvala in her most recent book of short stories
A Stronger Climate (1968) tells of the seekers: "Those people
who look to India for something that Europe fails to give them,
attracted by the stronger climate, the stronger colours, the
stronger personalities that they find there; they want emotionally
and spiritually to enrich themselves by their contact."

As Dubey, the foreign educated adviser in <u>Storm in Chandigarh</u> (1969) by Nayantara Sahgal is made to say, illustrating again the dilemma of the foreign educated Indian, and yet his basic awareness of his Indianness (p. 110): "It's a maddening state of affairs when you have to make an effort to know your own background...we are strangers to it because of our education and upbringing...yet we live with it and always shall." Indians know this, they know that it is only a thin glaze of Westernization that may succeed in fooling Westerners that they are all brothers under the skin, but their sad difficulty is to persuade their fellow countrymen still resident in India of this. As Sasthi Brata says (on p. 217 of <u>My God Died Young</u>): "Like the Englishman, the Indian is peculiarly proud of perpetuating certain traditions rather tenaciously while pulling an embarrassed face when taxed about them. Indeed he even at times achieves that degree of self-deception by which he can deny that the things he loves most actually exist in his country."

While we are considering this general problem of communication, translation, self-expression which does not distort, I think you might be interested to hear briefly how two Indians who saw England at first "through a glass darkly," through her literature, reacted when they saw her "face to face." Mrs. Dongerkery in <u>On Wings of Time</u>, feels that, "the written word transformed itself into a three dimensional panorama and enhanced the beauty of England." She had no feeling of distortion. Nirad Chaudhuri wrote <u>Passage to England</u> in 1959 after his visit to the country (which had come on the strength of the wide appeal of his autobiography, <u>The Autobiography of an Unknown Indian</u> (1951)). He had a great knowledge of the literature and history and some knowledge of its people, yet

> All this confidence vanished as soon as I landed on the ground and bewilderment took its place. I had no previous idea that things which were so familiar to me from pictures, which I could still identify as objects in outline could become so strange and different in their three dimensions, atmosphere and personality. As long as I remained in England a persistent trance-like effect never left me, and nothing seemed quite real, not even the human beings I was meeting. The only persons who appeared to be made of flesh and blood were the Englishmen I had known in India, all the rest glided like wraiths...I felt as I did partly because what I was seeing corresponded almost

preternaturally with what I had read about in books
and yet was infinitely more solid, tangible and
therefore more overpowering to the senses.

The literary mirror seems to have been a clear one, but
even so there is a shock. I do not think the literary mirror
through which the Westerner can see India is clear (with very few
exceptions); it is more like a fairground mirror that changes
at each step. And if Indians well read in fine English classics
feel bewildered with the reality of England how far can we with
our much shallower knowledge of India understand that society
when it is written about largely by partially alienated Indians?
I would like to quote from Modern Indian Literature (1968)
from an article by H.Y. Sharada Prasad (p. 206):

> The expatriate writer is naturally placed in a position
> far away from the details of usual cultural stimuli.
> Being far away from the context which strengthens him
> spiritually, he is forced to rely on memory which gives
> progressively diminishing flash-backs, resulting in
> increasing frequencies of the highlight. The necessity
> of response to such intermittent stimuli is urgent and
> therefore simplified.

On p. 212 he goes on to add, "The most significant result of
the impact (of the West) on Raja Rao seems to be the complete-
ness of his reaction away from it."

Since 1952 when I first became interested in the Indian
novel in English the trickle of works has increased to a flow,
and since 1966 (when my book was published)[1] this flow has
become a stream. I have managed to read most of those that
reached England despite many difficulties. Since I came here
I have learnt of others. Many more (mainly of the ill-written,
novelettish description) never get abroad except by accident.
(Two such are Trails of Glory by A.C. Biswas (1966) and
Gold in the Dust by S. Athogias (1960)).

The perspective is constantly changing as new writers
emerge to challenge old generalizations. As I. Baktiyar said
in 1964--I quote from The Novel in Modern India--"When
Bankim wrote the chief question was how to restore the national
self-respect. In Rabindranath's time it was how to bridge the
East and the West. In this dynamic age it is how to identify

ourselves with the common people." Now Indian English fiction
and poetry have been recognized as forming a significant part of
world literature in English (although it differs from Australian
English, for example, as for most writers it is the second
language), and within India, the Indianization of English has
gradually fixed it permanently in the socio-cultural setting.
D. N. Raghavacharyulu says "we have perhaps just begun to
settle down to the task [of criticism] after having overcome the
fallacies and inhibitions inherent in the pioneering process of
recognizing and identifying the uniqueness and distinctiveness
of the literature itself." The problem involves also the consideration of how the historical reality enters into the content of
works of art and gets transformed and transfigured...and also
the manner in which the creative statement once completed, the
work of art enters the cultural corpus.

> The importance, for example, of such a work as Raja
> Rao's The Serpent and the Rope cannot be judged by
> merely discovering and describing its particular
> context of the individual and the historical moment...
> in a sense these writers prepare us [i.e. Indians] for
> the aesthetic and creative transfiguration of our interest
> in the English language.

In 1962 K. R. Srinivasa Iyengar's work, Indian Writing in English
was a plea for these writings to be considered. Now because of
the great popular acclaim some of them have received and the
fact that they are valued as some kind of national quintessence
rather than as fiction there is a real danger of promoting a
self-conscious Indianness--I mean Indianness for its own sake.
In David McCutchion's words, the problem is how to be "neither
an imitation Westerner nor a picturesque Indian." The pre-
occupation with quintessence may, he thinks, prove a substitute
for the discipline of the novelist's craft and if you equate realism
with the West the tendency will be to excuse any sentimentally
idealized hero in an Indian novel as somehow "Indian" in conception.
Then a literature which might have been expected to bridge East
and West is in danger of turning uncritically back upon itself even
to the point of seeming to affirm that the less it is understood by
the West the more it is true to itself. The impression is inescap-
able that Raja Rao's The Cat and Shakespeare (1965) like The
Serpent and the Rope purports to reflect a different kind of mind

"not only outside Western categories but also beyond Western criticism." The mirror that the novel might be is deliberately clouded over by fumes of incense!

D.V. Raghavacharyulu on page 343 of Critical Essays on Indian Writing in English (1969) says, considering the novels as a whole, that "the creative moods vary from alienation to affirmation, from irony to despair, from humour to cynicism, from objective dispassion to indignant commitment, but, taken together, they splendidly orchestrate an imaginative version of the collective reality. To pass by these characteristic aggregates in the march of the literary sub-culture and to concentrate only on the successful works in isolation is to ignore the whole process of the passage of art into the consciousness of the culture."

I have looked over my list of those who write novels in English and viewed them from a slightly new perspective (as far as it is in my power to do so, being a specialist in no Indian discipline), asking whether they afforded to me a clear picture of India and, if not, why not. An interesting but not very surprising thesis emerged. It is those with the least direct knowledge of the West who provide us with the clearest mirror of India, e.g., R.K. Narayan. Those who inherit ability to understand both East and West, e.g., R.P. Jhabvala, can most clearly show up the interracial difficulties. Those who forsake any conventional idea of the novel form for the saga, the fantasy, the traveller's tale, or the biography, communicate more clearly because their task is easier, e.g., M. Anantanarayan, author of The Silver Pilgrimage (1961) or an older and Muslim novel, Twilight in Delhi by Ahmed Ali published in 1940 and republished in 1966, or Santha Rama Rao's thinly disguised autobiography, Remember the House (1956). Those who confine themselves to small, intimately known areas have the seeds of accuracy in them, e.g., S. Menon Marath, a native of Kerala, who writes about it in The Wound of Spring (1960) and The Sale of an Island (1968), and Mulk Raj Anand (in so far as he is concerned with Punjabis).

From the linguistic point of view those who approached English after education on the continent of Europe do better than those who studied English in England--they are not so self-

conscious. I am thinking here of Sudhin Ghose, author of
And Gazelles Leaping (1949), Cradle of the Clouds (1951),
The Vermilion Boat (1953), and The Flame of the Forest
(1955), and Raja Rao. Those whose work is imbued with
political or theosophical stances blur their communication.
Those who come from an urban cosmopolitan setting reflect
that setting and the conflicts of change felt in those circles.
It is only when there is not a studied choice of medium but
an inner compulsion which finds a more or less natural
outlet that we can hope for success.

Here is a list of some of the authors and details of their
contact with the West:

1. Mulk Raj Anand--educated partly in London and
   Cambridge
2. B. Bhattacharya--educated in London
3. Anita Desai--has one German parent
4. S.N. Ghose--was educated at Strasburg
5. Z. Ghose--was educated in England
6. R.P. Jhabvala--is of European Jewish origin and
   was educated in England
7. A. Lal--was educated at Oxford and may be of
   Anglo-Indian origin
8. Huthi Singh--was educated at Geneva
9. Khushwant Singh--was educated at London
10. Menon Marath--is a native of Kerala but is a resident
    in England
11. Kamala Markandaya (a pseudonym for Mrs. Taylor)--
    is, I understand, married to an Englishman
12. Balachandra Rajan--had a brilliant academic career
    in England
13. Santha Rama Rao--was educated first in England,
    later in America
14. Raja Rao--was educated at Montpelier and the
    Sorbonne, and has lived in France and America
15. Nayantara Sahgal--a niece of Pt. Nehru's, was
    educated in England, later in America.

Krishna Kripalani says of these novelists and their works
that they have not yet succumbed to the morbid spirit of cynicism,
violence, and sex obsession which has become the bane of their
highbrow counterparts in some countries of the West. There
(according to C.D. Narasimhaiah) widespread affluence and the

resultant conformity of the individual and a pervasive standard-
ization of society is driving the Western novelists in search of
new themes and attracting readers to Patrick White of Australia,
Chinua Achebe of Nigeria, V. S. Naipaul of the West Indies,
R. K. Narayan, Raja Rao, and Santha Rama Rao of India.

From this list I have omitted the Hindu author resident in
Trinidad, V. S. Naipaul, who cannot properly claim to be within
my terms of reference. I have also omitted R. K. Narayan for
the very good reason that he may be unique.

Here then is a wholly Indian writer whose first contact with
the West, apart from its literary influence, came in the wake of
his fame. He is a rarity in other respects too. Notice what the
Indian reporter says of him in an interview in India News,
June 8th, 1968: "He never made speeches on the novelist's
craft or on Tagore and modern Indian Literature. He did not
seem to be bothered much about the writer's duty to society.
He observed and wrote and saved time for his art." I should
like to read you part of the paper on English in India[2] which he
delivered at the University of Leeds in 1964 as it may interest
us all:

> When I was five years old I was initiated into the
> mysteries of letters with the appropriate religious
> ceremonials. After being made to repeat the name of
> God, I was taught to write the first two letters of the
> alphabet on corn spread out on a tray, with the forefinger
> of my right hand held and propelled by the priest. I was
> made to shape the letters of both the Sanskrit and the
> Tamil alphabets, because it was the language of the
> province in which I was born and my mother tongue.
> But in the classroom neither of these two languages was
> given any importance; they were assigned to the poorest
> and the most helpless among the teachers, the pundits
> who were treated as a joke by the boys, since they taught
> only the "second language" the first being English as
> ordained by Lord Macaulay when he introduced [sic]
> English education in India. English was important and
> was taught by the best teacher in the school, if not by the
> ruling star of the institution, the headmaster himself.
> The English Primer itself looked differently styled from
> the other books in the school bag, with its strong binding
> and coloured illustrations--those were days when educa-

tional material was imported and no one could dream of
producing a school book in India. Thus from the Sanskrit
alphabet we passed on directly to the first lesson in the
glossy primer which began with "A was an Apple Pie"
(or was it just Apple, I don't remember); and went on to
explain, "B bit it" and "C cut it". The activities of B and
C were understandable, but the opening line itself was
mystifying. What was an Apple Pie? From B's and
C's zestful application, we could guess that it had to do
with the ordinary business of mankind, such as eating.
But what was it that was being eaten? Among fruits we
were familiar with banana, guava, pomegranate and grape,
but not apple (in our part of the country), much less an
apple pie. To our eager questioning, the omniscient one,
our English teacher, would just state, "It must be stuff
similar to our idli, but prepared with apple." This
information was inadequate and one popped up to ask,
"What would it taste like? Sweet or sour?" The teacher's
patience now being at an end, he would say, "Don't be a
nuisance, read your lessons", a peremptory order which
we obeyed by reciting like a litany "A was an Apple Pie".
We were left free to guess, each according to his capacity,
at the quality, shape, and details, of the civilization por-
trayed in our class books. Other subjects were also
taught in English. We brooded over arithmetical problems
in which John did a piece of work in half the time that Sam
took, and when they laboured jointly, when would the work
be completed? We also wrestled with bushels of oats and
wages paid in pounds, shillings and pence, although the
characters around us in actual life called themselves Rama
and Krishna and handled rupees and annas rather than
half-crowns and farthings. Thus we got used to getting
along splendidly with unknown quantities in our studies....

For an Indian training in the classics begins early in
life. Epics, mythology, and Vedic poetry, of Sanskrit
origin and of tremendous antiquity, are narrated to
everyone in childhood by the mother or the grandmother
in a cosy corner of the house when the day's tasks are
done and the lamps are lit. Later one reads them all
through one's life with a fresh understanding at each stage.
Our minds are trained to accept without surprise characters of godly or demoniac proportions with actions and
reactions set in limitless worlds and progressing through

an incalculable time-scale. With the impact of modern
literature we began to look at our gods, demons, sages,
and kings, not as some remote concoctions but as types
and symbols, possessing psychological validity even
when seen against the contemporary background. When
writing we attempted to compress the range of our observation and subject the particle to an intense scrutiny.
Passing, inevitably, through phases of symbolic, didactic,
or overdramatic writing, one arrived at the stage of
valuing realism, psychological explorations, and technical
virtuosity. The effort was interesting, but one had to
differ from one's models in various ways. In an English
novel, for instance, the theme of romance is based on a
totally different conception of man-woman relationship
from ours. We believe that marriages are made in heaven
and a bride and groom meet not by accident or design but
by the decree of fate, the fitness for a match not to be
gauged by letting them go through a period of courtship
but by a study of their horoscopes; boy and girl meet and
love after marriage rather than before. The eternal
triangle, such a stand-by for a Western writer, is worth-
less as a theme for an Indian, our social circumstances
not providing adequate facilities for the eternal triangle.
We, however, seek excitement in our system of living
known as the joint family, in which several members of
a family live under the same roof. The strains and
stresses of this kind of living on the individual, the
general structure of society emerging from it, and the
complexities of the caste system, are inexhaustible
subjects for us. And the hold of religion and the conception of the gods ingrained in us must necessarily find a
place in any accurate portrayal of life. Nor can we over-
look the rural life and its problems, eighty-five out of a
hundred Indians being village folk.

English has proved that if a language has flexibility
any experience can be communicated through it, even
if it has to be paraphrased sometimes rather than conveyed, and even if the factual detail, as in the case of
the apple pie, is partially understood. In order not to
lose the excellence of this medium, a few writers in
India took to writing in English, and produced a literature
that was perhaps not first-class; often the writing seemed
imitative, halting, inapt, or awkward translation of a

> vernacular rhetoric, mode, or idiom; but occasionally
> it was brilliant. We are still experimentalists. I may
> straight away explain what we do not attempt to do. We
> are not attempting to write Anglo-Saxon English. The
> English language, through sheer resilience and mobility,
> is now undergoing a process of Indianization in the same
> manner as it adopted U.S. citizenship over a century ago,
> with the difference that it is the major language there,
> but here one of the fifteen listed in the Indian constitution.
> I cannot say whether this process of transmutation is to
> be viewed as an enrichment of the English language or a
> debasement of it. All that I am able to confirm, after
> nearly thirty years of writing, is that it has served my
> purpose admirably, of conveying unambiguously the
> thoughts and acts of a set of personalities, who flourish
> in a small town located in a corner of South India.

Here is an honest craftsman and it is not surprising that his
mirror is clear, if small.

Raja Rao too has made a mirror. In his hands the English
language is a fine tool and his fluent manipulation of it is the
more refreshing for its French influences. The mirror shows
the working of his own mind and personality and--I quote from
David McCutchion, at p. 77--

> our involvement in it is an extraordinary and revealing
> experience. At any rate I know now intimately and
> convincingly what it feels like to be a Western educated
> Madrasi Brahmin, a thousand years old or three, a
> pilgrim on the road to Travancore which is anywhere
> and nowhere, another red spot in the mind. And Rama,
> after all, is not transcendent however misty, he is very
> real--and also familiar. It suddenly struck me that the
> type is not confined to India at all. Marius the Epicurian!

Ruth P. Jhabvala writes in her own second language as one
detached from the Indian scene yet firmly resident in it. She is in
an excellent position, and has the impulse and the gift of writing to
show us the incongruities of character and situation resulting from
an intermixing of East and West in an urban cosmopolitan society.
Her handling of the theme is essentially that of a writer of social
comedy. She presents certain situations and follows the train of
thought and feeling in each character, creating for the time being

an illusion of complete sympathy and endorsement. But the juxtaposition of characters and the incongruity of a particular mode of thinking pitched against a specific situation makes the reader perceive ironic undertones. The representation of the married life of Esmond and Gulab in Esmond in India (1958) is quoted as an example of this in N. Meena Belliappa's article in The Literary Criterion, Winter 1966, no. 3, in 'Indian Women Writers of Fiction in English' (p. 18):

> You see things from Gulab's point of view, participate in her languor, share her relish for hot spicy curries smuggled in from her mother's house and eaten with her fingers, sitting on the floor, sympathize with her dislike of furniture which seems to her to restrict freedom of movement, understand her reluctance to go into smart society...and then you see it all as Esmond does; a smartly furnished modern flat superimposed with the animal presence of stupid, slovenly Gulab, whose interests in life do not go beyond sleep and food. It is then that you sense the tonal layers operating in the seemingly matter of fact non-partisan narration and see the contrast, the incompatibility, of two individuals who are as unlike each other as the ways of living they represent.

Needless to say Mrs. Jhabvala's work finds wide acceptance both here and in India.

Anita Desai's work interests me. I should like to know more about her personal life and her education. English may well be her first language. I understand she has not been outside India -- or had not when her first two novels Cry the Peacock (1963) and Voices in the City (1965) were written. She is engaged in, or may even have completed, her third. She seems to me to write for the very good reason that she is compelled to, and although the background is again the urban middle class one we expect, and she knows, we are quickly involved with the individual characters, who are not placed firmly against a background of India there to move in traditional patterns, but are seen in depth. Her first novel tells of the oncoming madness of a young wife. In the second--against a highly evocative background of Calcutta-- three members of one family relate their experiences. She holds my attention. I do not think her view of Indian life is a distorted one; but what is the life she is viewing?

To return to the mirror. From Indians of a cosmopolitan Western highly trained background we hear of an India where mixed marriages are accepted, where dams are built, where experts of all nationalities meet and mix in new towns or are involved in new projects, where social life might seem almost to exist on the American pattern. From the homesick native of Kerala we hear (with certain beauties heightened by nostalgia) about his birthplace. From those who are compelled to write because of their loneliness and rootlessness or the speed of change which has overtaken them we get an impression of an eroded past, an unhappy present and a doubtful future. Each author, to whichever category he belongs, provides a mirror only of his own section of Indian life. I contend, in conclusion, that we should now be concerned, now that we have a criterion whereby we can distinguish these writers, not to treat writers in English as a group contrasted with writers in the regional languages, but rather to select for our own purposes the mirror we need.

The mirror provided by the "westernized writers" reflects a marginal section of India. Because of India's scale even her margins are broad. Because the section is marginal, protagonists of writing in regional languages resent these materials being mistaken for substantially representative Indian fiction, and they are right. But if we expect the problems of Indians to continue, problems between the two worlds as well as problems wholly within the Indian world, this marginal literature will continue. And if we, too, decry mannered and artificial writing and encourage more natural expression of genuine emotional response to those two worlds and to the conflicts between them-- conflicts of which the individual writer is a focus--we shall in our small way (as consumers) help that marginal literature to be, and to continue to be, a respectable contribution to English literature quite apart from its status within the greater body of Indian literature.

Notes

1. The Modern Indian Novel in English. A Comparative
   Approach. (Brussels, Institut de Sociologie, Université
   Libre de Bruxelles, 1966) (Collection du Centre d'étude
   du Sud-Est Asiatique, 3). I reserve for the present my
   rejoinder to the polite, detailed, but unappreciative
   review of this book by Lothar Lutze in "Literarische
   Fremdenführung...", Intern. Asien Forum 1 (1970),
   no. 1, pp. 130-142.

2. From J. Press, ed., Commonwealth Literature; Unity
   and Diversity in a Common Culture (London, Heinemann,
   1965), pp. 120, 122-3.

Gandhi: A Twentieth-Century Anomaly?

by

J. H. Broomfield

Early one misty morning in January 1941, a bearded figure, dressed as a Muslim, slipped away from a house on a Calcutta back street to begin what has become an epic journey in modern Indian history. Eluding the police and ultimately the British military on the frontier, he made his way across North India into Afghanistan, where he arranged with difficulty to be taken to Moscow and on to Berlin. There he persuaded the Nazis to provide him with the resources to raise an Indian regiment, which he hoped would spearhead the armed liberation of his homeland. When it appeared that the Japanese were likely to reach India before the Germans, he made another journey, by submarine to Southeast Asia, there to raise an Indian National Army. His troops saw action against the British in Burma before their leader died in an air crash in 1945.

This heroic figure was, of course, Subhas Chandra Bose, and his life story is in many ways typical of the twentieth-century revolutionary nationalist. Western-educated, with a university degree, he went in his late teens to the imperial metropolis, London, to compete successfully for a place in the ruling Indian Civil Service. At his moment of triumph, however, he renounced the opportunity, and returned to India to join the new mass movement of resistance to British rule. In his twenties he organized militant youth brigades, reaching the height of his popularity during the civil disobedience campaigns from 1930 to 1932. He advocated the violent overthrow of the British, and led paramilitary formations in displays of opposition to their imperialism. He was arrested, imprisoned and externed for long periods, but from his gaol cell in exile he continued to exhort his countrymen to rise in revolt against their oppressors.

In Bose we can see the likeness of many other twentieth-century revolutionaries: Mao, Ho, and Sukarno in Asia; Kenyatta in Africa; Madero and Castro in Latin America; Venizelos, Husseini, and Grivas in the Eastern Mediterranean; Trotsky, De Valera, Tito, and Hitler in Europe. All were practitioners of the politics of militant confrontation, and all earned their periods of imprisonment or exile. All shared an ambition to mobilize sectors of their societies to effect the overthrow of perceived imperialisms, internal or external. All were attracted by military styles of organization and discipline, and all had faith in the efficacy of violence.

How striking the contrast if we consider Mohandas Karamchand Gandhi. During that same civil disobedience campaign of 1930 in which Subhas Bose led his young storm troopers against the police, we find Gandhi on his Dandi salt march: a walk of 200 miles through village India to the seacoast to make salt as a symbolic gesture of resistance to British rule. What a quaint figure we see in the photographs: a skinny, knobbly-kneed little man, dressed in a loin cloth, granny glasses perched on his nose, barefoot, setting forth with only a walking stick to assist him on a trek which would daunt most men of sixty. Here was a man leading a great political movement with watchcries of truth, love, self-suffering, abstinence, and non-violence. Surely anomalous watchcries for the twentieth century with its dynamic emphasis upon revolutionary uprising and violence? Perhaps Gandhi is an anomalous figure in this century? "In an era that takes matters of religious faith lightly," Susanne Rudolph has written, "it is difficult to consider a man who is suspected of saintliness."[1] Yet it is Gandhi, not Subhas Chandra Bose or the many other Indian proponents of violence, who is best known outside, as well as inside, India.

Let us recap the main features of Gandhi's life to draw out the characteristics of his ideals and achievement. He was born in Kathiawar, an isolated northwestern peninsula, where his father was a princely state official. The environment in which he was raised was one of orthodox Hinduism, and he was strongly influenced by the quietous principles of Vaisnavism and Jainism. His was an educated but not, we may fairly say, an intellectual family. He was put into that most favored of professions for the nineteenth-century Indian elites, the law, and, as few Indians in that century could hope to do, he was enabled to go to Britain in 1887 for extended legal education.

Gandhi's first months in London were cold, lonely and uncomfortable (as his photographs of the period suggest: flannel suit, starched shirt, Victorian high collar, and all). It was not until he abandoned his legal studies and began to associate with a vegetarian, pacifist group that he discovered some warmth and friendship in that alien city. It was in this company that he rubbed shoulders with such European minds as Tolstoy, and the American, Thoreau. The mixed metaphor of shoulders and minds is appropriate, for Gandhi does not appear to have gained any deep understanding of these thinkers. They influenced him, but mainly by reinforcing established beliefs. The basis of his philosophy is to be sought within his own Indian traditions.

In 1891, having belatedly resumed his legal studies and passed the bar examinations, Gandhi returned to Bombay, where he was an instant and spectacular failure as a barrister. Rising in court to plead his first case, he found himself at a loss for words, and he was quickly demoted to office paper work. In 1893 his firm received a lucrative but routine request for legal counsel from a member of the Indian community in the Transvaal. The partners looked around for their most dispensable clerk-- and despatched Mr. Gandhi.

The experience in South Africa, though in origin so humdrum, was to work a transformation in Gandhi's life--a transformation so spectacular that it may be compared with that of Saul on the road to Damascus. Gandhi arrived in South Africa to be met with racial discrimination of a kind he had never experienced in India or Britain. It shook his faith in the fundamental justice and goodwill of the British imperial system. For a time he was at a loss for a course of action, but finally in May 1894, goaded by the imminent disenfranchisement of his compatriots in Natal, he formed the Natal Indian Congress. The inarticulate young lawyer was gone; in his place stood an outspoken and courageous crusader against racial injustice.

For the next 20 years, up to the outbreak of the First World War, Gandhi worked in South Africa. In this land far from India, step by step he fashioned his new revolutionary technique, to which he gave the name satyagraha: "soul force," which he contrasted with "brute force." His basic principle was ahimsa: non-violence. Non-violence in thought as well as deed, for Gandhi drew on a philosophical tradition which does not recognize that hard distinction between thought and action with which we are familiar in the West. Angry thoughts injure the thinker as well as those against whom they are directed. So Gandhi insisted that love, not hatred, must be the guiding principle of political, as well as personal, action. One must empathize with one's adversary, seeking the good in him and his cause, and trying to eradicate whatever is evil--in self or opponent. The aim in politics, Gandhi emphasized, is to help one's opponent escape his error, as much as to advance one's own cause. The objective must be to heal social wounds, to establish a new basis for reconciliation and positive political action in the future; not to antagonize and polarize. "My experience," he wrote, "has shown me that we win justice quickest by rendering justice to the other party."[2]

This did not mean that injustice from others should go unresisted. Indeed, Gandhi emphasized that non-violent resistance to oppression was a duty. Urging his fellow Indians in South Africa to united action in defense of their communal rights, his call was: "Not to submit; to suffer."[3] Again he drew upon the traditions of his native Gujarat in applying to politics a technique of moral suasion used there in familial and mercantile disputes. The method was for the aggrieved party to shame his adversary and win sympathetic support for his cause by a display of self-abnegation, most commonly fasting. With this model in mind, Gandhi devised a succession of non-violent confrontations with the South African authorities. The issues were diverse, and time and place varied greatly, but there was a common aim: to provide those in power with opportunities to demonstrate the injustice of their regime by forcing them to retaliate against limited, non-violent and symbolic acts of protest.

Gandhi achieved a surprising number of victories, but the long-term gains for the South African Indian community were negligible. For this reason the real significance of this period of Gandhi's work must be sought in the experience it gave him: as an organizer, tactician and publicist. His trips to India and Britain in search of finance and support provided enduring contacts for his later work with the Indian National Congress, and the attention his movement attracted in the press assured him of fame among politically-aware Indians. He left South Africa in 1914 after a striking success against the Union Government. His opponent of many years, the Minister of the Interior, Jan Smuts, breathed a sigh of relief. "The saint has left our shores," he wrote. "I sincerely hope for ever."[4] It proved to be so.

Gandhi in India had bigger fish to fry--if one may use so inappropriate a metaphor for a vegetarian! The Indian nationalist movement to which he returned, and in which he was clearly determined to play a role, had developed rapidly in the preceding decade. If, for comparison's sake, we use the familiar categories of American Black nationalism, the Indian movement had developed from its late nineteenth-century NAACP stage, of a liberal union of right-thinking men, through a period of marches and sit-ins, to economic campaigns to "Buy Black," accompanied by cultural revivalism ("Black is Beautiful"), and finally to the revolutionary call to arms: "Burn, Baby, Burn." As one might expect, such radical developments had split the Indian National Congress. Growing disunity and the failure of the Congress leaders to win mass support, had convinced many nationalists of the need for a structural reorganization of their movement.

Into this situation Gandhi came with striking advantages. He had an established public reputation, but, unlike other prominent figures, he was free of factional identification. Moreover, he was an experienced organizer, with his own patented technique of agitational politics. Circumspect as ever, he bided his time. He spent the war years extending his network of political contacts, but steadfastly resisted the temptation to be drawn into their factional squabbles. He chose his own distinctive point of entry into the Indian political arena, initiating a peasant satyagraha against the British indigo planters of northern Bihar in 1918. The indigo industry he attacked was uneconomic, and had been maintained only by blatant exploitation of the peasant cultivators. His satyagraha was a rapid and complete success, and its publicity precipitated him into the front rank of nationalist leaders.

For Gandhi it was a dictum of politics that an unjust regime is bound to enlarge the area of conflict by its over-reactions to protest. The months following his Bihar movement seemed to prove him right. Disturbed by industrial and peasant unrest, and with a weather-eye on Bolshevik successes in Russia, the Government of India insisted upon arming itself with legislation to extend its wartime powers of summary action against suspected conspirators. Gandhi responded with a call to the Congress to organize nation-wide hartals (general strikes). April 1919 brought mass protests in many cities of northern and western India, and, when violence erupted in the Panjab, a jittery British administration retaliated brutally. In the bitter aftermath, Gandhi was able

to persuade the Congress to accept his blueprint for reorganization, and his leadership of a mass campaign of non-cooperation.

It is instructive to observe the elements Gandhi emphasized
in the program he advanced, for it will give some measure of the
principles which were to guide his three decades of political work
in India. In the first place he proposed that all participation in
the activities and institutions of British Indian government should
cease, and that Congressmen should devote themselves to the
construction of national institutions: "a government of one's own
within the dead shell of the foreign government."[5] Resistance,
non-violent and symbolic, might be offered to particular acts of
British oppression, but the really important work was in national
reconstruction. For the nation as for the individual, Gandhi
taught, salvation could be gained only by internal reformation.
Society had to be rid of its evils, especially those of dissension
and human exploitation. As a first step he called for reconciliation between religious communities, and he took up the Khilafat
issue as a means of cementing Hindu-Muslim unity. He also
demanded that caste barriers be broken down and that the untouchables be accepted into the body of Hinduism. Congressmen
of all castes should work with the Harijans (the "Children of
God," as Gandhi called them) to help them rise from their
degradation.

Similarly, there had to be an end to economic oppression.
Gandhi was adamant that self-government for India would be a
travesty if the mass of the people were not freed from the exploitation of capitalists, landholders, and moneylenders. The
nationalist movement had to be the people's movement, to benefit
the mass of the people. He insisted that Congress demonstrate
its concern for the welfare of the Indian poor by adopting a program of economic rehabilitation. Congressmen should leave
their urban professions and go into the villages to start cottage
industry. The local manufacture of cotton cloth should be revived.
The spinning wheel should become the symbol of India's new life,
and the wearing of khadi (homespun) a gesture of the nation's
rejection of imperialism.

In its initial stages in the early months of 1921, the first
non-cooperation movement was a remarkable success. The
unprecedented numbers participating in the agitation--Muslims
as well as Hindus--raised serious alarm among British officials.

To the perplexity of many of his colleagues in the Congress hierarchy, however, Gandhi seemed to value opportunities for confrontation with the Government less than those for popular political education and social reform. His insistence on continually shifting the focus of the movement, and his prohibition of what to others seemed logical areas of agitation, e.g. industrial disturbances, frustrated even some of his closest followers. In part these shifts reflected his mature judgement of the need to keep the British off-balance; in part they were the product of a determination to maintain his personal domination of the movement; but, most of all, they reflected his deep concern to preserve non-violence. It was the conviction that he had failed to do this that led to his sudden call in February 1922 for an end to the agitation.

Gandhi initiated two other great campaigns and a host of minor actions in the years before independence. Always he put major emphasis on ethical considerations, insisting doggedly that he alone must be their arbiter. Always he was unpredictable in his tactical decisions, and in his timing of the final withdrawal. As a consequence, there were some who became totally exasperated with his leadership--amongst the most outspoken being Subhas Chandra Bose. We need not follow Gandhi step by step through these years, but we must surely ask: how could he retain his following despite such apparently eccentric political behavior? The question is the more intriguing when we realize that on a number of occasions he withdrew from active politics for five or more years at a time, and yet was still able to emerge at his chosen moment to resume the leadership of the national movement.

One answer is that Gandhi was a phenomenal scribbler, a fact readily verified by a count of the number of volumes of his khadi-bound collected works, now threatening to engulf all but the largest libraries. His polemical writings filled his own newspaper and the columns of many others, year in and year out. He produced books on politics, religion, social organization, and his own life. During his great campaigns, his scribbled battle orders poured from every halting place; and from his ashram during his years of retreat the flow of advice, praise, cajolery, and (forgive the heresy) moralizing never ebbed. Gandhi knew the value of a good communications system, and he spared neither himself nor his assistants in his efforts to keep in touch.

He also knew the value of good lieutenants. It is paradoxical that while Gandhi was not particularly responsive to criticism (being too assured of the quality of his own judgement), he was willing to tolerate strong differences of opinion amongst his associates. Indeed it should be put more positively: he worked hard (often through painfully devised compromises) to prevent disagreements over ideology or strategy from driving able men and women out of the Congress. As a consequence he retained the loyalty of a remarkable number of talented and forceful workers.

As these two points suggest, Gandhi was an organizer par excellence. We should not be misled by the sainthood conferred upon him by popular mythology (as by Professor Rudolph and General Smuts), into thinking of him as some impractical, dreamy visionary. This was the man who took the ramshackle Indian National Congress of the second decade of the century, and rebuilt it as an effective nationwide organization, extending from a full-time working central executive, link-by-link to representative committees in virtually every district of British India. At the high points of participation during the civil disobedience campaigns, the formal organization reached even to the villages. Though periodically weakened by the removal to prison of its office-bearers, it survived to provide independent India with a nationwide institution parallel to, and reinforcing, the governmental structure.

Another of Gandhi's personal attributes -- one which he undoubtedly shared with other great politicians -- was extraordinary physical and mental stamina. The seemingly frail old man could outwalk, outsit and outtalk others half his age. We have amusing accounts from the second Round Table Conference in London of British Cabinet Ministers wilting perceptibly as Mr. Gandhi, calmly and quietly, talked on into the small hours of the morning. His slow, tireless methods drove foes, and sometimes friends as well, to distraction.

Lastly, Gandhi had what we can only describe as an amazing mass appeal. He was known to, and revered by, millions in urban and rural India like no other figure in historic times. Wherever he went the news of his coming spread far beyond the reach of the mass media. How could this be? The easy thing to say is: because of his charisma. But that is no answer; merely a rephrasing of the statement about his mass appeal. Gandhi was a master of symbolism, and here we may have a key. To say he was "a master of symbolism" is to make him sound more manipulative than I would intend. Rather, he had a keen sense of the political, social and ethical fitness of a variety of symbols and symbolic acts.

Let us take some examples. The Dandi salt march of 1930, already mentioned, was one of his most brilliant, yet simple, symbolic successes. All men need salt, and in many places in India salt can be produced with the simplest equipment, or even scraped up from dried pools or marshes. The British Indian Government, however, levied a tax on salt and prohibited its unlicensed production. Obviously an attack on this restriction would be universally popular, and would serve as an indictment of a regime that taxed the basic needs of its pitifully poor colonial population. Brilliant in conception; equally brilliant in execution: a long march through village India, gathering thousands of supporters, drawing the attention of the world press to the moment by the sea when the imperial policemen would be forced to arrest India's most revered leader, and unmanageable numbers of his adherents, simply for lighting a fire and heating a pan of salt water.

Gandhi's choice of the spinning wheel and khadi to represent the revitalized Congress, was a similar attempt to find symbols that would have emotive appeal across the many levels of Indian society. To the urban professional classes, it was a call for a return to a more pure and traditional way of life. Discarding imported cloth offered them a way to make a visible sacrifice for the cause, while striking a blow at British economic domination. It also offered them an opportunity (not welcomed by all) for a symbolic union with the masses by donning common garb. For the peasantry, the spinning wheel was among the most sophisticated of their familiar instruments of production, and one which had frequently provided a marketable product to supply an income above their minimum needs. For generations past the sale of homespun had brought them a few good times and good things, but all too often of late their spinning wheels had lain disused, unable to compete with factory-manufactured goods. In Gandhi's symbols they saw the promise of a restoration of a more just order.

Gandhi himself was a living symbol. His life style expressed a traditionalist philosophy. To many he appeared as the humble ascetic, the pure man of the soil, fearless of his environment because his own physical survival meant little to him. Confident and courageous, yet devoid of all defensiveness, even the defensiveness of blustering arrogance. This idealized stereotype owed much to the Indian tradition of the ascetic leader, a tradition in which Gandhi himself believed implicitly. He was at pains to project the image of the brahmachari (celibate). Although his rejection of worldly comforts was sometimes ostentatious (a puckish disciple is credited with the comment: "You have no idea how much it costs to keep Mahatmaji in the style of poverty to which he has become accustomed"[6]), there can be no question that he was thoroughly sincere in his conviction that strength came through a renunciation of sensual indulgence. He accepted traditional Indian theories of physiology and psychology which hold that the bodily essences, giving physical, mental and moral strength, are dissipated through such outpourings as sex and anger, but increased by pure foods, particularly vegetables and milk products, and through disciplined meditation. Gandhi shared this belief with the vast majority of his fellow Hindus. They saw that he was a disciplined brahmachari, and they had no difficulty in understanding the source of his superior stamina and moral virtue.

He earned for himself the title, Mahatma: great soul. It is a title he disclaimed, but significant nonetheless, for it suggests a link with an Indian tradition of religious leadership which has been disregarded in measuring Gandhi's impact on twentieth-century India. This is the tradition of the religious ascetic combining spiritual instruction for a peasant community, with the leadership of that community in rebellion against its oppressors: against (in Eric Hobsbawm's words) the "special form of brigand,"[7] the Government, and against the lesser, but regrettably more familiar, brigands: tax collectors, policemen, landlords, and moneylenders. Many Hindu folk tales and many of the most popular epics concern such rebel gurus, leading the fight against injustice. In more recent times, under Muslim rule and in the nineteenth century, there are many historically recorded cases of religious teachers, sufis and bhaktas particularly, providing leadership for local revolt. Gandhi could easily be understood by the peasant community as a great leader, a mahatma, in this tradition of protest.

As Eric Wolf has observed: "Simplified movements of protest among a peasantry frequently center upon the myth of a social

order more just and egalitarian than the hierarchical present."[8]
Gandhi, by attacking the hierarchical present, by symbolizing a
resistance to the economic oppressions worked by instrusive
modern technology and its accompanying innovations in the organization of labor, by using the language and symbolism of the popular
Hindu tradition, mobilized rural mass India in a way that would
never have been possible had independence from Britain been the
sum total of the Indian nationalist movement. It was his genius
to have seen the need, and to have provided the means, to link
together the urges of India's peasant masses with the struggle
to expel the foreigner.

Here we touch the tragic core of Gandhi's life. He used
symbolism brilliantly. He was a master of emotive religious
imagery and the historical myths associated with his religion.
But in a multi-religious and multi-cultural society, such an emphasis on one tradition, even if it is an unconscious emphasis
expressed through a life style, must inevitably give offense to
some groups. We cannot be surprised, given the structure of
Indian thought in the early twentieth century, that attempts at
mass mobilization would involve the use of Hindu symbols, but
equally we must expect the alienation of non-Hindu communities,
most notably the Muslims, a quarter of all Indians before 1947.
The Muslims felt increasingly threatened by Indian nationalism,
and the Mahatma--for all his non-violence--was not a reassuring
figure. Gandhi devoted his last ten years to a struggle to heal
the wounds opened between Islam and Hinduism in the mass political movements of the century. It was tragic irony that he should
be assassinated in 1948 by a Hindu nationalist who blamed him
for the concessions to the Muslims that made possible Pakistan.

Let us return to the original question: was Gandhi a twentieth-
century anomaly? Certainly he was out of step with much else in
the twentieth century, but he was intentionally so. It was not that
he was unaware of what was occurring around him. He emphasized
"soul force" as a counter to what he saw as the omnipresent,
twentieth-century brute force. He emphasized non-violence for a
society he believed to be far too violent. He was not saying, as
many have mistakenly suggested, that non-violence was the Indian
tradition. Rather, he lamented that India had many violent traditions, and warned his contemporaries not to let those traditions
dominate. He charged them to take the most noble of their tra-
ditions--non-violence--and work to ensure its dominance of their
national life.

This invites the retort that he had little success: India, after Gandhi, remains a violent place. Similarly, many will question the general effectiveness of non-violence as an agitational strategy, and they can cite numerous instances of its failure. It would be foolish to suggest that non-violent movements are always victorious, but that claim could scarcely be made for violent struggles either. Perhaps, if we could draw up a score sheet, we would find that failure was no more frequent in non-violent than in violent agitations, and I suspect we would discover that in the former, means less often distorted ends.

What Gandhi contributed with satyagraha was an alternative model of revolutionary action. He extended the range of political options available to the twentieth-century activist. This was no mean achievement.

Perhaps Gandhi was an anomaly in another way: as a traditionalist leader in a modern world? Not so, I would argue. If we properly understand our twentieth-century world we shall expect to find traditionalist leaders all about us. Such understanding, however, has been made difficult by the false dichotomy many social scientists (and journalists in their wake) have drawn between tradition and modernity. Modernization, we have been told, implies moving away from the traditional. On the contrary, I would argue that tradition is not something dispensed with as one becomes modern. Tradition is the cement that binds society together. If it is hard and inflexible it may prevent change, or change may crack the cement and shatter the society. This has happened, but rarely. Usually the cement is flexible, for tradition is a malleable commodity. In the hands of traditionalist leaders it can be bent and reshaped in adapting the society to modern demands. Insight comes from understanding and interpreting the continuity of tradition: the strengths or weaknesses of diverse traditions for various social and political purposes. Because of our acceptance of the false dichotomy between tradition and modernity, we have equated modernization with change, and neglected the equally valid equation between tradition and change. We have been taught to regard traditionalist leaders as reactionaries, when in fact many, like Gandhi, have been vigorous proponents of change. Frequently they have been the most effective "modernizers," for they have understood the importance of presenting change in comprehendable, i.e. traditional, forms.

There is a final point to be made about Gandhi's relevance to the twentieth century. He recognized the critical need to deal with the problems of the peasantry -- still a majority of the world's population, though so often treated as an anachronistic survival. We have already pointed to his attempts to evolve an economic program for the Indian nationalist movement that would relieve the economic hardships and social dislocations inflicted on peasant communities by industrialization. Through his criticism of urban elitism in the Congress, and, more importantly, through his own labors in rural reconstruction, he attacked the disfunctional and debilitating status inferiority imposed upon the cultivator by the cult of urban civilization. In his reverence for the tradition of the village panchayat (council of elders), and in his utopian hopes for the ultimate withering away of the central state structure, he faithfully reflected the peasantry's hostility to that "cold monster," the state,[9] whose baffling complexity grew with every advance in communications technology. In his insistence that the Congress not become the inheritor of the institutions of British administration, he was trying to prevent in India what has happened almost everywhere else in the ex-colonial world: the transfer of the power to exploit the peasantry from an urban-centered imperialist regime, to an urban-centered nationalist regime. Far from being an anomaly in his twentieth-century world, Gandhi was wrestling (however unsuccessfully) with a crucial problem of that world: the construction of an economic and political order in which the peasantry could have a full role.

Notes

1. Susanne Hoeber Rudolph: "The New Courage. An Essay on Gandhi's Psychology", World Politics, vol. XVI, no. 1, October 1963, p. 98.

2. My Experiments With Truth (Ahmedabad, second edition 1940) p. 225.

3. See W. K. Hancock: Smuts. The Sanguine Years, 1870-1919 (Cambridge, 1962) p. 329.

4. Ibid., p. 345.

5. C. F. Andrews paraphrasing Gandhi. Letter to Rathindranath Tagore, 6 September [1920], Andrews manuscripts, Rabindra Sadana, Visva-Bharati.

6. Attributed to Sarojini Naidu. (To my acute embarrassment, I have been unable to find the reference to this quip.)

7. Eric Hobsbawm: Primitive Rebels. Studies in Archaic Forms of Social Movement in the Nineteenth and Twentieth Centuries (Manchester, 1959) p. 36.

8. Eric R. Wolf: Peasants (Englewood Cliffs, 1966) p. 106.

9. Eric R. Wolf: Peasant Wars of the Twentieth Century (New York, 1969) p. 294.

Images of India

by

Rhoads Murphey

I want to try to evoke a series of aspects of India and to ask
you to consider the question of perspective. I've worked in some
way or another with India for twenty-five years, I've lived there
for three or four years at different times, and I've read a good
many books. But I still find a need for perspective; if I didn't
what work I do with India would be not only much more difficult
but much less valid. I find it awkward to use the phrase South
Asia; by "India" I mean the subcontinent, including, without any
sense of denigration, Pakistan. One of the many things which
one can label this India as being is diverse -- extraordinarily
diverse. One almost despairs of generalizing about it. That
in itself suggests the usefulness of varied perspectives.

Let me begin with one which makes a good curtain raiser to
an effort at understanding other cultures. Aldous Huxley took a
trip around the world in the early 1920's, spent a long time in
India, and wrote a very amusing and, I think, a very wise account
of what he found. This is how he finishes his book, called
Jesting Pilate:

> So the journey is over and I am back again... richer by
> much experience and poorer by many exploded convic-
> tions, many perished certainties. For convictions and
> certainties are too often the concomitants of ignorance...
> I set out on my travels knowing, or thinking I knew, how
> men should live, how be governed, how educated, what
> they should believe...I had my views on every activity
> of life. Now, on my return, I find myself without any of
> these pleasing certainties...The better you understand
> the significance of any question, the more difficult it
> becomes to answer it. Those who like to feel that they

are always right, and who attach a high importance to
their own opinions, should stay at home. When one is
traveling, convictions are mislaid as easily as spectacles. But, unlike spectacles, they are not easily
replaced.[1]

For those who don't find this kind of an experience unsettling,
it is one of the strong arguments in favor of studying another
culture. India is perhaps more rewarding than any if only because
of its immense variety and the ease with which it can destroy the
pleasing certainties which Huxley talks about as being easily
mislaid when one confronts different ways of doing things and is
obliged to acknowledge that they work, although they are radically
different from one's own. But, of course, everyone who tries to
get perspective like this or who is put in a situation where perspective might be expected to follow doesn't achieve it. Westerners, Americans in particular, are especially well-buttressed,
case-hardened, against having their own values or perceptions
affected by the differences that they observe. Differences are
labeled simply as aspects of inferiority and not as occasions for
the observer to examine himself and the way his culture does
things, if only out of intellectual interest.

Probably the most famous and perhaps the greatest novel
written by a foreigner about India is E.M. Forster's A Passage
to India, which revolves around the extent to which people can
live in another culture and remain sublimely unaware of what it
is they are observing and experiencing. That can of course
happen to people without their going to India. It's quite possible
to acquire a lot of information and still totally to misunderstand.
India is so very different and so very varied, so shockingly
different in many respects from what Americans are accustomed
to, that there is a danger of ending up as Mrs. Moore does in
A Passage to India. She is seeing India always, Forster says,
as a frieze, never as a spirit. She sees its color, she sees
something of its excitement, but she doesn't really see what's
going on. India is an immensely colorful country--colorful in
both a literal and a figurative sense. Perhaps in a way that is
unfortunate, because it may draw one's attention away from what
is more important. In any case, here is Mrs. Moore riding
in a dog cart, looking at the scenery,

while the true India slid by unnoticed. Color would
remain--the pageant of birds in the early morning,
brown bodies, white turbans, idols whose flesh was
scarlet or blue--and movement would remain as
long as there were crowds in the bazaar and bathers
in the tanks. Perched up on the seats of a dog cart,
she would see them. But the force that lies behind
color and movement would escape her. [2]

Perhaps if we are aware of the risk of this kind of thing
happening, we are better able to protect ourselves against it,
to look for something more than the superficially attractive,
exotic, colorful aspects of India, or the superficially repellant,
frightening, upsetting aspects of India, which are equally
observable, and look for something behind them. It is super-
ficialities of the latter sort that I want to read you something
about now from I think what must be an astute observer of India,
someone who did understand what was going on--a reporter for
the Manchester Guardian:

A quarter of the way round the globe a black cloud
comes rushing down the street. Before you can take
shelter great gouts of rain stab the broken pavements.
The Indian monsoon is on. Only a week ago everyone
and everything was parched and gasping. The very
crows were gasping. Now, however sticky the air, the
rice fields are sprouting emerald green. Peasants
swish about in the mud. There will be a harvest.

To many people India's poverty seems to be a stumbling
block. I couldn't go there--too depressing. Others
try to shame us into proper awareness of our sinful
affluence and our duty to aid poorer countries and are
apt to say things like 'Most people in Calcutta live below
the threshhold of hope.' How much do such people know
of life or of history? Man is tough. Calcutta is a place
of great suffering, but of surging life and of hope. Not
even the concentration camps, after all, could drive
most people below the threshhold of hope. And in Calcutta
few take life lying down. The difficulty in talking about
India is that we do need to concern ourselves with poverty
and its radical problems, but it will be of no use if we
do so in a mood either appalled or patronizing. For one
thing, we shall put off the Indians. For another, we shall

mislead ourselves. What happens to 500 million Indians is obviously important in the world at large, but it doesn't follow that we should despair if they fail to develop in the way we think best--as a unitary state or whatever. I am glad that Indians do not go to jail, as others elsewhere do, for thinking or speaking or writing unpopular thoughts, and I shall be glad when everyone in India has enough to eat. But like every society, India will develop in her own way. We can like it or dislike it, and say so. We ought to join in her development, not out of charity, but because it is one of the most stirring of all happenings in the world today. India seems to me a crucible where a very large part of mankind is living out its own transformation. [3]

The main point I would like to extract from what this gentleman says (apart from the sermon he includes at the end, which I would underline) is that it is very important, if one is going to understand India or indeed any so-called developing country, to avoid being trapped by the kind of instinctive reactions which many Americans, in particular, find themselves generating-- loathing or despair. They look at the streets of Calcutta, which admittedly is an extreme example, or at an Indian village, which seems so different and so poor that an American may wonder how people can survive there: India is hopeless, it's so poor, it's so different from the rest of us. It can't ever become...what they would like to say, I think, is civilized, but what they really mean is rich.

There is an assumption on the part of many Westerners, and especially of many Americans, that to be poor is somehow to be subhuman, uncivilized, that material wealth is essential to happiness. It really isn't true. It wasn't true even in this country a hundred and fifty years ago. When the United States began it was a poor country. That was one of the things which gave it its distinctiveness, and, indeed, something which the people who established this country took as one if its virtues, together with its lack of pretension. America was contrasted, to its favor, with Europe, where people were rich and powerful. India is poorer, however one chooses to measure this, than the United States was in 1776. But the point is that wealth is not everything; because someone is desperately poor by American standards doesn't mean that he may not be creative, happy, productive, imaginative, well worth examining and understanding, and just as important, if one is going to try to strike a balance of that kind in the affairs of the world, as anybody else. This is the kind of attitude which many

Americans find it hard to adopt. They are appalled by what they see in material disparity between India and their own experience. It's a mistake, of course, to judge any culture by the standards of another culture. India is itself--immense, varied, ancient, and enduring. This kind of unseeing or wrong-seeing may be just as misleading as the kind of unseeing or wrong-seeing which Mrs. Moore and other characters in A Passage to India illustrate.

What is the real India like? It is like a thousand things, of course. But something like three quarters of India's people still live in villages, and the village world is thus the major part of the culture. It is not easy for outsiders to understand, but it's necessary if one is to pretend to understand what India is made of. Let me read a brief passage from Behind Mud Walls, a sympathetic account by two American sociologists who tried to penetrate a village in order to understand it, and in the end succeeded. Here is a description of their first approach:

> We sat on the running board of our car and contemplated the village across the road. We had chosen Karampur as being reasonably typical of the villages in our section of the United Provinces. [The former colonial name for Uttar Pradesh.] We had secured credentials from higher quarters and had been officially introduced to the patwari, the village accountant in the employ of the government. We had found an old mango grove and had set up tents for our helpers and our two small sons. Now we were ready to study the village. But would the village permit itself to be studied? Certainly, it gave no sign of welcome.

> The irregular, high, rain-furrowed mud walls which faced us might have been mistaken for a deserted fortress. No dooryards, no windows were there to give glimpses of family life. Nothing but blank walls and more walls, so joined that it was often difficult to tell where one man's house ended and his neighbor's began. Dark doorways, patted into shape by hand, were the chief indications of separate dwellings. Directly opposite the entrance to our grove was a high-arched doorway, once imposing, now about to collapse. Behind it were more blank walls. The only breaks in the weather-beaten barrier were narrow lanes leading back into the village. These, too, were bordered by walls....Beyond the far end we could see carpenters at work in a lane. A few extraordinarily thin cows wandered in from

> the fields and disappeared through the dark doorways,
> or down the narrow alleys. After some time a woman
> emerged from one of the doorways, a water jar on her
> head and another on her hip. She slunk close to the wall
> and hurried around a corner as though afraid of attracting
> our attention. [4]

It's pretty clear that this was a place which didn't want to be
studied. It was a world apart and wanted to stay that way. But
after a long period, the two Americans won the confidence of the
villagers; they began to listen to and take part in a long series
of explanations by the villagers of why they behaved the way they
did, why they were unfriendly to outsiders, why they valued their
well-defended village world:

> "In all of our self-protective activities," a villager says,
> "each of us is not thinking of his own self. No villager
> thinks of himself, apart from his family. He rises or
> falls with it. In the cities families are scattering. But
> we need the strength of the family to support us. We do
> not trust the outside world. The village has survived the
> coming and going of many landlords and many rulers by
> remaining inconspicuous and providing its own
> sustenance." [5]

Hence, of course, the mud walls. It's not just mindless
hostility or unfriendliness which is responsible for the kind of
exterior the village puts to the outside world but rationality,
which the villagers in time explain. Once inside the barriers,
into a world which would be physically an affront to the eyes and
nostrils of most Americans, it turns out in time, once one makes
the effort to understand it, that people are living for the most part
very happily. They are poor, and are periodically in serious
trouble as a result of their poverty. But they don't see their
world, and therefore it shouldn't be seen by other people, as one
of limitless misery, which is the way in which external observers
would instinctively be inclined to see it when they look simply at
its superficial manifestations. In any case, the villagers place
a high value on their own way of doing things and on the little
world in which they live--and, like most people, a low value or
a lower value on other worlds, particularly the cities. They
know a little bit about cities, some by hearsay, some by direct
observation. And what they have to say about the difference
between the village and the city reflects a very Indian point of

view. The village is still seen through a kind of golden haze in
the minds of a great many Indians, whatever its actual realities,
which are a mixed business as life is everywhere in any part of
the world. The village has a special aura--that is where man
really belongs, that is where all of the right values fall into place
correctly. In the cities, this is not possible. People are perverted
or limited. The kind of life which God intended us all to live is
possible only in the village:

> "People in cities have little that we do not already have.
> They may have better and more schools...They keep
> their lanes cleaner than we do, and some of them have
> cleaner habits. They have more convenient medical
> services. Some day we shall have all that they have.
> In addition, we have plenty of fresh air, which they lack,
> and plenty of sunshine. Our children have more than
> enough room to run and play in safety. We do not have
> to go to a crowded dirty bazaar to buy our grain or
> vegetables or our fruit or our milk. In the city vege-
> tables and fruit are half withered, the milk is half water,
> and the ghi is seldom pure. We have our own food, fresh
> from our fields...We are not driven, the way men in the
> cities seem to be. We take time to enjoy our families
> before we go out to work in our fields. After work we sit
> with our friends. We enjoy telling jokes on ourselves
> and on others. There is much to laugh over. Perhaps
> we are just as well off without watches; actually we want
> them more for show than for use. Those who live by
> them become servants, not their own masters. We
> know the time by the sun and the stars, and we know
> how much work must be done....We are not afraid of
> work. Perhaps you hear one or another of us singing as
> we pass your house on the way to our fields...We do not
> have the cinemas and the loudspeakers that make city
> life exciting, but we have our own good times. We
> enjoy every special festival, and there are plenty of them
> during the year...Of course, some city men have easy
> jobs, sitting at desks in offices or sitting on the floor of
> small stores...[but] most men in cities work in mills.
> That is not for us. We want to be free...We have our
> worries, but they are not as bad as those of city people.
> When we stop to think about it, we have a good deal in
> our favor."[6]

This is of course a somewhat idealized view, even though it is coming directly from a villager. But it does suggest that Indian peasants are not stupid because they choose to live in villages surrounded by mud walls or because they have certain habits and circumstances which we do not share and which we feel we have rejected in favor of something better. The peasant has a different set of perceptions and a different set of values with which he is at least as content as we are with ours. In the current atmosphere of self-criticism in the West, which is probably a healthy development after a century or so of self-confidence in the "modern world" and its ability to solve the human problem, one may guess that the Indian peasant may have done as well in this sense as people who live in cities.

Village life has its hard side too, of course. The Indian environment is a dramatic and difficult one, the principle difficulty being the violence of its climate. It is hot, but it is also dry. Heat and drought usually come to a climax just before the onset of the monsoon rains, which is the most dramatic and often most violent aspect of the Indian environment. The arrival of the monsoon is tremendously exciting, like a catharsis, and also like the returning of life to a scorched, parched land. But it may bring disaster rather than promise for the peasant. The monsoon may be over-violent and destroy his work, or it may be long delayed and crops may die in the field before the rains finally arrive, when they may do more harm than good by producing floods instead of watering the rice seedlings or the wheat seedlings for which the peasant has awaited the rains until it was too late. There is a passage illustrating this aspect from the peasant point of view in Kamala Markandaya's magnificent novel Nectar in a Sieve, set in a village in South India:

> Nature is like a wild animal that you have trained to work for you. So long as you are vigilant and walk warily with thought and care, so long will it give you its aid; but look away for an instant, be heedless or forgetful, and it has you by the throat. Ira [her daughter] had been given in marriage in the month of June, which is the propitious season for weddings, and what with the preparing for it, and the listlessness that took hold of me in the first days after her departure, nothing was done to make our hut weatherproof or secure the land from flooding. That year the monsoon broke early with an evil intensity such as none could remember before.

It rained so hard so long and so incessantly that the
thought of a period of no rain provoked a mild wonder.
It was as if nothing had ever been but rain, and the
water pitilessly found every hole in the thatched roof
to come in, dripping onto the already damp floor. If
we had not built on high ground the very walls would
have melted in that moisture. I brought out as many
pots and pans as I had and we laid them about to catch
the drips. But soon there were more leaks than we had
vessels. . . . Fortunately I had laid in a stock of firewood
for Ira's wedding and the few sticks that remained
served at least to cook our rice, and while the fire
burnt, hissing at the water in the wood, we huddled
round trying to get dry. At first the children were
cheerful enough--they had not known such things before. . . .
but Nathan and I watched with heavy hearts while the
water rose and rose and the tender green of the paddy
fields sank under and was lost. "It's a bad season,"
said Nathan sombrely. "The rains have destroyed
much of our work; there will be little eating done this
year." At his words, Arjun [the boy] broke into doleful
sobs and his brother Thambi followed suit. They were
old enough to understand but the others, who weren't,
burst into tears, too, for by now they were cramped and
out of humour with sitting crouched on the damp floor;
and hungry since there was little to eat. . .As night came
on--the eighth night of the monsoon--the winds increased,
whining and howling around our hut as if seeking to pluck
it from the earth. Indoors it was dark--the wick burning
in its shallow saucer of oil gave only a dim wavering
light--but outside the land glimmered, sometimes pale,
sometimes vivid, in the flicker of lightning. Towards
midnight the storm was at its worst. Lightning kept
clawing at the sky almost continuously, thunder shook
the earth. I shivered as I looked--for I could not sleep,
and even a prayer came with difficulty. "It cannot last,"
Nathan said. "The storm will abate by morning." But
even as he spoke a streak of lightning threw itself down
at the earth. There was a tremendous clap of thunder
and when I uncovered my shrinking eyes I saw that our
coconut palm had been struck. That too the storm had
claimed for its own. [7]

That was the beginning of a long series of disasters which over-
took that particular family, unfortunately not untypical, perhaps
especially in parts of South India where there has been for many
centuries a vicious combination of mounting over-population and
physical disasters. But the drama, the excitement, the violence
of the Indian environment, although chronically hard and periodically disastrously hard on the 75 or 80% of the population who
must live by working the soil, has its positive kind of an excitement for everybody, including those who are harmed by it, but
especially for those who live in the cities and are one step
removed from the problems of the farmer. There is also a
symbolism about the monsoon which is woven into the fabric
of Indian life and of Indian imagery in a way which may be
possible to appreciate only if one has lived through a few Indian
seasons and seen the extent to which almost in an unspoken way
people associate the change of the seasons and their dramatic
violence with the great cycle of birth, decay, death, and rebirth
which are particularly vividly felt and expressed in India. In
an agricultural system, these things are obvious and basically
important. But when the monsoon comes to the city also, it
means an end to the great period of heat and therefore a moment
of enormous relief for everyone and a dramatic symbol that the
wheel has come around once more, the cycle is being repeated.
Here is another description, from a positive point of view, by
another Indian novelist, in this case from Punjab, describing
the coming of the monsoon:

> There is a flash of lightning which outshines the day-
> light. The wind fills the black sails of the clouds and
> they billow out across the sun. A profound shadow falls
> on the earth. There is another clap of thunder. Big
> drops of rain fall and dry up in the dust. A fragrant
> smell rises from the earth. Another flash of lightning
> and another crack of thunder like the roar of a hungry
> tiger. It has come! Sheets of water, wave after wave.
> The people lift their faces to the clouds and let the
> abundance of water cover them. [This is, in fact, quite
> a literal discription of what often does happen right in
> the middle of the big cities in India when the monsoon
> comes, particularly if it has been delayed.] Schools
> and offices close, all work stops. Men, women, and
> children run madly about the streets, waving their arms
> and shouting. With the monsoon, the tempo of life and
> death increases. Almost overnight grass begins to grow

and leafless trees turn green. Snakes, centipedes,
and scorpions are born out of nothing. The ground
is strewn with earthworms, ladybirds, and tiny frogs.
At night, myriads of moths flutter around lamps.
They fall in everybody's food and water. Geckos
[little lizards which crawl on the wall and the ceiling]
dart about filling themselves with insects till they get
heavy and fall off ceilings. Inside rooms the hum of
mosquitoes is maddening. People spray clouds of
insecticide, and the floor becomes a layer of wriggling
bodies and wings. Next evening, there are many more
fluttering around the lamp shades and burning themselves
in the flames. [8]

This is a vivid and appropriate description of the process
which is not only actually taking place but, in the minds of many
Indians, being symbolized--birth, decay, death, rebirth, the
great wheel of life. The Indian environment seems to epitomize
it especially sharply. Indian appreciation of the monsoon may
be part of a more generally Asian acceptance of nature and belief
in the rightness of a harmony between man and nature. Harmony
with nature implies adjusting to and admiring what is greater and
more powerful than one's self. It is neither possible nor appropriate for man to fight against nature. He must accept it, the
good and the bad, as part of the natural order of the universe,
just as he must accept the realities of death and of life, and he
must remain close to and sensitive to the natural world in a
harmonious relationship. Such a conception of man's role and
his place in the universe contrasts with modern Western or
American attitudes. It is involved in part in the Gandhian
opposition to the industrialization of India and in the idealization
of the village. Cities are seen as discordant, as soulless, as
attempting to disrupt, or at least to alter, traditional patterns
of harmony, as divorcing themselves from nature.

The notion of harmony is also involved in the Indian doctrine
of non-violence, something which Albert Schweitzer has described
in his own terms as reverence for life. Religious or philosophical
concerns form another very important aspect of Indian life, a
more important part of Indian culture, and of the thinking of most
Indians, than is the case not only in the United States but I suspect
nearly anywhere else in the world. Religion is not something
which is normally as readily separable from the rest of people's

lives as tends to be the case in the modern Western tradition. Nor is it something which is properly seen merely as ritual. Although ritual is important in India, the metaphysical and philosophical inner reality is more so. In some ways, contemporary India may suggest comparison with medieval Europe in these terms, when essentially religious ideas meant a great deal to most people. Religious pilgrimages still take place in India regularly; people no doubt take part in them for many of the same reasons that Chaucer's pilgrims walked to Canterbury. But among those reasons, in Chaucer's time too, there was a genuine religiosity involved. In India, that is present as well, to at least the degree that it was in medieval Europe. Here is a description of a pilgrimage by Irawati Karve, an Indian anthropologist; it might almost be a slightly Indianized <u>Canterbury Tales</u>. It has many of the same elements--crowds, amusements, the opportunity for social chitchat with friends, relatives, or people from another village, the excitement of a special occasion, and yet the very pious religiosity which goes along with it as well:

> People impatient to get out were pushing me from behind; people anxious to get in pulled me out. Somehow I landed on my feet on the dusty platform. I gathered the few packages and made my way out of the railway station through a crowd. The reasons for the crowds became clear: today was the day of the weekly market, and the "god" on his journey had reached this town to make a day's halt. My guide and I picked our way through heaps of millet and wheat and rice, through pots and pans, through bales of cloth and saris, toys and hand-mirrors, vegetables and sweets--everything displayed on both sides of the road. Farther on, there were amusements--the revolving cradles and merry-go-rounds, gramophones shrilling loudly, a snake-charmer, a troupe of tight-rope dancers.

> Today, as once every year, the image of Saint Dnyaneshwar rested for one day here on its fifteen days' march from Alandi in the Poona district to Pandharpur in the Sholapur district. People from far and near had flocked to pay respects to the great saint. Whole families had come. They would "visit" the "god", then buy in the market, amuse themselves, and go back. Thousands walked from Alandi to Pandharpur with the image of the saint, some joined later on the way, some like me hiked

the twenty miles from Poona over the hills, then joined
the others at this station and walked for twelve days over
the plains. We cut through the crowds. My companion
pointed toward the open space...I looked up and saw
above the heads of people a dirty white canvas tent, with
a shining golden pinnacle. The saint was represented
by silver images of his feet...My companion, a well-
known preacher and devotee, was given a seat among
the men. I was led inside to a room for the women...

"We must hurry," said the first voice. "Pots and
pans have to be scoured and washed and packed in the
truck before the god starts moving."

We got up and stood by the road. I heard the trumpet.
The procession had started. Our dindī came along. Tai
bent down and took up the dust on the road. God's saints
were passing today on this road. The dust under their
feet was sacred. I too dipped my finger in the dust and
put it to my forehead. The ritual was followed every day.
We joined our own group. The drum gave the rhythm, the
lute strummed the tune, the men with two small cymbals
tied to a string around their necks marked time and sang
one of the multitude of sectarian songs composed since
the thirteenth century.

> The quality of compassion is to love--
> To love without thought of return--
> As a mother loves her child.

Easier said than acted! How is it possible? Or--is
it so impossible? That sparrow which built its nest,
which fed the little ones all day long--what did it expect
in return? It mourned pitifully when my cat ate the
fledgling, but what did it lose? Can one order one's love
at all? Does love ask one's permission before it appears?
It weaves itself into the warp and woof of the heart without asking permission; the threads are pulled all the
time this way and that, and may cut deep. Then men
cry out with bleeding hearts, "Oh God! Please rescue
us." Not only the love of the mother, but all love is
without any thought of gain; that is why it is so painful. [9]

It is not that non-Indians haven't thought some of these same things
before and some may even think them now, but that essentially

religious questions and essentially religious commitments are
a much more important part of daily life in India than almost
anywhere else. It would be an incomplete picture of Indian
culture if that aspect of it were not at least briefly mentioned.

I've talked so far almost entirely about what I suppose one
should call traditional India --at least, I've talked about it in a
timeless way--quite intentionally. But I want to finish by trying
to relate the India of the timeless past to the India which is now
in the process of emerging, or is working out its own transformation as the gentleman from the Manchester Guardian put it.
Let me read from part of a speech made by Mr. Nehru to the
Constituent Assembly in 1946, on the eve of Indian independence.
In some ways it is a very British kind of speech and a British
kind of a scene; Nehru thought of himself and talked about himself
as half an Englishman, half an Indian as a result of his own
experience and education. The beginnings of self-government in
India came long before independence and were set in the British
mold. But what Nehru is talking about and the kinds of uncertain-
ties he is expressing are, I think, an eloquent effort to relate the
India of timeless tradition to the India which is now emerging:

> As I stand here, Sir, I feel the weight of all manner of
> things crowding upon me. We are at the end of an era
> and possibly very soon we shall embark upon a new age;
> and my mind goes back to the great past of India, to the
> 5000 years of India's history, from the very dawn of that
> history, which might be considered almost the dawn of
> human history, till today. All that past crowds upon me
> and exhilarates me and, at the same time, somewhat
> oppresses me. Am I worthy of that past? When I think
> also of the future, the greater future I hope, standing
> on this sword's edge of the present between the mighty
> past and the mightier future, I tremble a little and feel
> overwhelmed by this mighty task. We have come here
> at a strange moment in India's history. I do not know,
> but I do feel, that there is some magic in this moment
> of transition from the old to the new, something of that
> magic which one sees when the night turns into day and
> even though the day may be a cloudy one, it is day after
> all, for when the clouds move away, we can see the sun
> again. Because of all this I find a little difficulty in
> addressing this House and putting all my ideas before it
> and I feel also that in this long succession of thousands
> of years, I see the mighty figures that have come and

gone and I see also the long succession of our comrades
who have labored for the freedom of India. And now
we stand on the verge of this passing age, trying,
laboring, to usher in the new.[10]

It would be a great mistake to judge India by the present
alone and certainly to judge India by the problems which are
all too easy either for an Indian or an outside observer to pin-
point. Troubles between India and Pakistan, squabbles within
the Congress Party, violence over the language issue, periodic
food shortages and then food gluts, all kinds of distressing
growing pains or simply the kinds of chronic problems which any
large group of people, however homogeneous or heterogeneous,
confront when they try to work and live together. One of the
difficulties in trying to understand something about India is that
the only news worth printing is bad news, dramatic news -- someone is shot, someone starves, someone calls someone else a
liar in parliament, someone publishes a scare report of famine
or epidemic. From a newspaperman's point of view, it may be
difficult to make a story out of a recitation of things that are
going well. But even if we acknowledge that all of the dreadful
things are really happening and that several of India's problems
are genuinely frightening, India has been around for a very long
time. Throughout that long time it has been an immensely
vigorous place, creative, productive, changing, rising and falling
if you like, but staying in business. It isn't going to go away
because a few politicians trade bad words with one another or
because there is chronic disorder in Calcutta or because most
Indians are poor and are going to stay poor by American standards.

If one were to characterize contemporary India as a whole,
allowing for its many problems but also for the equally dramatic
positive things which are less often reported, and throwing in a
large measure of things which are neither good nor bad but which
are just happening as this particular society evolves and changes,
perhaps the most important features are vigor and vitality. I
am thinking in part of what has been happening in the Indian
economy and in the Indian agricultural system, particularly in
the last four or five years as the attractiveness of innovation is
finally becoming apparent to peasants who previously, and for
good reasons, were distrustful of change. Change is now something at least to be examined if not eagerly adopted, rather than
something to be resisted without question. I am thinking also of
what has been happening in the political arena in India since

independence and particularly since the death of Mr. Nehru, when virtually everyone, and many people inside India also, were prophesying political disaster. India could never handle the succession problem, could never manage the demanding system of parliamentary government with a free press and a largely illiterate and impoverished electorate. But it has been done, and with characteristically Indian vigor. India does not seem in any way to me to be a hopeless case, or one about which one should be appalled or repelled. In confronting a dismaying array of problems in the economic and political spheres since independence, India has rebounded from each crisis. The Indian tradition is as old as civilization, as Nehru reminds us; it has enormous staying power, and it is not going to disappear. Certainly one of the most exciting aspects of the contemporary world is the effort of this ancient culture, now about one fifth of humanity, to come to its own terms with the twentieth century, and to devise its own distinctively Indian solutions.

Notes

1. Huxley, Aldous. Jesting Pilate, London, 1927, p. 223.

2. Forster, E.M. A Passage to India, London, 1924, p. 35.

3. Cave, Andrew. Manchester Guardian Weekly, July 26, 1968.

4. Wiser, William H. and Charlotte. Behind Mud Walls: 1930-1960, Berkeley, 1963, pp. 1-2.

5. Wiser, pp. 122-23.

6. Wiser, pp. 228-29.

7. Markandaya, Kamala. Nectar in a Sieve, New York, 1955, pp. 57-59.

8. Singh, Kushwant. Mano Majra, Bombay, 1959, pp. 27-29.

9. Karve, I. "On the Road: A Maharashtrian Pilgrimage," Journal of Asian Studies, 22 (1962), pp. 13-30.

10. de Bary, W.T., ed. Sources of Indian Tradition, Volume II, New York, 1964, p. 350.

Printed and bound by CPI Group (UK) Ltd, Croydon, CR0 4YY

13/04/2025

14656537-0005